THE MOST INSPIRING BASEBALL STORIES FOR KIDS

30 INCREDIBLE BASEBALL TALES FOR YOUNG READERS

NOAH PRESS

CONTENTS

CHAPTER 1
BABE RUTH MAKES ONE FINAL YANKEES APPEARANCE

The world legend in sport is often overused. Many fans use it just for players that they like, or the current star of the team. However, some people who have played professional sports do genuinely deserve the title and term 'legend' to be used. One such person is Babe Ruth. Babe Ruth is one of the best baseball players of all-time. He was a hero for the Boston Red Sox and the New York Yankees. His transfer to the Yankees set about turning them into the biggest baseball team in the world – at the expense of the Red Sox.

Ruth's career was a hugely successful one, and is one of the greatest baseball careers ever seen. However, like all legends, his career finally came to an end. Across 22 seasons in the MLB, Ruth saw huge success playing from 1914 until 1935. 'The Bambino' is probably the greatest Yankee of all-time. A left-handed pitcher and a slugging superstar, few people in the history of baseball have lived up to his incredible achievements. He was also one of the first five members to the Baseball Hall of Fame.

In his career, he broke many records – many of which still stand to this day. He had a batting average of .342, and managed 2,873 hits in his amazing career. He was also the father of the 'Curse of the Bambino' that we have spoken about before. While kids can find out everything about his amazing career, many do not know about his final appearance at the Yankees Stadium in New York.

Ruth retired from playing in 1935, playing for the Boston Braves at the end of his career. Despite being keen to eventually become a manager, Ruth was not ready to finish his career until he played for the Braves in 1935. The team was struggling to get fans in the door, and so Ruth was signed to try and help get more people to turn up and see the last hurrah of one of Boston – and baseballs – greatest ever.

His first game brought about 25,000 people into the game, and Ruth helped the Braves win 4-2 against the New York Giants. This included a highly impressive two-run home run. However, his age and the poor quality of the team meant that he eventually left the Braves with his final appearance being against the Philadelphia Phillies. Sadly, they lost the game and it meant that his final game was a defeat.

The Braves went on to a poor 10-27 run to end the season, and finished the season 38-115 which is regarded as the worst winning percentage of any team in National League history. Things fell apart for the Braves, and Ruth retired quietly. He was brought into the Hall of Fame in 1936, the first of five members. Despite being interested in becoming a manager, though, Ruth was never offered a baseball management position. He expected to one day get a chance to manage one of his former teams, but the offer never formally arrived.

Sadly, Ruth's personal lifestyle choices had gone against him. Team owners did not want to hire a person as manager who had enjoyed the lifestyle that Ruth did. However, many other successful managers of the time – such as Bobby Valentine – enjoyed exciting lives away from baseball without being given the same criticism for their personality. For many, Ruth was treated badly by the sport once his playing days were over.

His next appearance at the Yankee Stadium came in 1939, when he appeared to give a speech for his teammate and friend Lou Gehrig who was being forced to retire young. Unable to even get a job on the radio, Ruth played lots of golf and appeared in random exhibition games. His last game at the Yankee Stadium came in 1943, when he played as part of the Army-Navy Relief Fund game.

Not being able to get a job with his beloved Yankees, though, hurt Ruth and he became very sad. He continued to play golf, though, which he saw as the best way to stay fit and still have some fun. He also took part in various charity golf events, but still longed for some kind of involvement in the game of baseball. That, though, would never come.

Sadly, many years of being left behind by the team meant that Ruth was simply not happy. He found it hard to retain any kind of connection to the game, but life changed for Ruth in 1946: he was diagnosed with a serious illness. His time left was short, and he wanted to have the chance to say goodbye to his former team before his time ran out.

So, on June 13th 1948, Babe Ruth stepped out at Yankee Stadium for one more time. The event was to help mark the 25th anniversary of the stadium opening, and also to retire the number three in honour of Ruth. A 25th anniversary dinner for the 1923 team was held, and Ruth was asked to attend given all that he had done for the team in his playing days. Sadly, he was too sick to attend.

However, he arrived at the Yankee Stadium clubhouse and was very sick. Ruth and the remaining members of the team were brought out to the stadium to see the fans one more time, and all of the players were given the chance to have their name applauded by the crowd. When Ruth's name was called out last, though, the stadium erupted with celebration at his amazing career.

Ruth moved toward his teammates in the middle of the stadium, with 50,000 fans there to give him one final farewell. He was given a baseball bat to use as a cane, and a tired Ruth waved his Yankees cap to the crowd. Ruth gave a brief speech to the crowd, saying that made him proud to be back with his teammates from their successful time together.

Ruth sadly missed the exhibition game that was held in honour of the team, and left the Yankees stadium for the last time. This would be the final time that Ruth appeared at the Yankees Stadium, as he sadly left the world in August of the same year. For fans there that day, though, the chance to say goodbye to one of the best players to ever hold a bat was important.

The day, though, marked one of the saddest in the history of the Yankees. The end of a legendary career and life.

CHAPTER 2

PETE GRAY'S YEAR IN THE MAJORS

For baseball fans around the world, a hero is something that every fan has. Someone that they can look up to and relate to. Someone who has achieved a special feat just by making it as a professional baseball player. Some players, though, are remembered for their ability to even make it to the Major Leagues in the first place. One player who fits this example perfectly is Pete Gray.

If you have not heard of Pete Gray, then he is someone worth knowing about. Born on March 6th, 1915, Gray was a unique player. He is, at the time of writing, the only player in the history of Major League Baseball to make a career in the game with only one arm. He was noted for being an impressive draw for the crowd, who were keen to see how someone with one arm could play baseball professionally. The following story follows his year within the Majors.

Gray always wanted to be an outfielder, and always wanted to play the game despite losing his arm as a child. Having only one arm would stop 99.9% of people from ever having the chance of playing the sport they love. However, Gray managed to build a career for himself in the Minor Leagues playing for a few teams. His most success came with the Memphis Chicks, though, where he made his name as the Southern Association's Most Valuable Player in the 1944 season.

Despite only having one arm, fans and players loved Gray. He was very impressive, able to maintain a batting average of .333 and also a stolen-base record of 63. He was loved by the fans who saw someone who worked with what they had. Despite only having one arm, Gray was still able to be a big contributor to his team. He was someone who the fans loved, too, for his commitment to the game.

He was even nicknamed "The One Armed Wonder" by the press, who were hugely impressed by his ability to play. He enjoyed success in the Minor Leagues for around six years. He was referred to by most as a courageous athlete, someone who was willing to go above and beyond to simply enjoy the dream of being a baseball player. However, nobody thought that he would ever get the chance to play in the Major Leagues. Across his Minor League career up until he got the chance to move on, he played for some good teams including the Trois-Rivieres Renards and the Memphis Chicks.

His big break, though, came in the 1945 season. His contract with the Chicks was bought out by the St. Louis Browns, who had reached the World Series in 1944. He joined the team on a $4,000 salary, and was given the #14. In his season with the Browns, he played left and center field positions and played 77 games. He managed a batting average of .218, and a .958 fielding percentage in center field.

His first hit in the Major Leagues came on April 17th, 1945, when he managed a single against the Detroit Tigers. His life's dream, though, had always been to take to the field of the Yankee Stadium and play for – or against – the New York Yankees. This happened on the 20th of May, when he played in a double-header match at Yankee Stadium. He managed to pull off five hits as the Browns managed to beat the Yankees on both occasions – 10-1 and 5-1, respectively.

However, as the year went on, it became clear that Gray's one-armed nature was limiting his ability to be a success. For example, he was unable to hit breaking pitches. With only one hand, he was unable to change the timing of his swing and opposition pitchers began to hit him with curve balls. This made him an easy player to play against for the other team, and by September he was beginning to get less game time.

His final game in Major League Baseball came on 30th September, 1945. He also had a tough relationship with many of his teammates, who felt like he was holding them back. Having been the American

League champions the year before, the Browns felt like they would have a chance at doing it again – and some of his teammates felt like Gray was slowing them down from playing their best.

In the games that he did play, Gray's team went 35-42. The games he missed, they managed a successful run of 46-28 – so there was a big difference in results when he played and did not play. Some cynics at the time said that he only was given a game because it was helping to increase attendances for the Browns, as people wanted to see the One Armed Wonder for themselves.

At the end of the season, the Browns finished third in the table and missed out on their repeat pennant. Brown was cut from the team for the next season, where they went on to finish in seventh place. In fact, the year with Brown was the final winning season that the Browns enjoyed before they were shipped up and moved away to Baltimore in 1954.

However, his success in baseball had been used as an inspiration to many other disabled people across America. Gray, for example, was used as an example to army soldiers who have been injured during the Second World War. The fact he was able to make a career for himself and play a year in the Major Leagues was seen as inspiring to many. He spent a lot of time visiting army hospitals and those who had been hurt during the war, giving them encouragement.

He returned to the Minor Leagues from 1946 until 1949, and his career finished in 1949 outside of exhibition games in the 1950s. Gray was the focus of a TV movie and also a biography about his life and achievements, which helped him to feel good about his success.

His glove is now held in the Cooperstown National Baseball Hall of Fame and Museum, and he was also brought into the Shrine of the Eternals in 2011. Through sheer force of will and talent, Gray enjoyed a year in the Major Leagues that many others never had. And while it was only one year, it is one of the most memorable years in the history of Major League Baseball.

CHAPTER 3
THE BLACK SOX SCANDAL

In baseball, many of the stories about players are moments of heroic success. Players coming through challenges to win their team the World Series. Players battling back from injuries and hardship to win titles and glory. However, what makes Major League Baseball so interesting is the fact that the league has such a unique history when it comes to success and failure. Many moments have taken place in the history of baseball that, while negative, are important.

The good and the bad is what makes the league what it is today, and unfortunately baseball has been home to many different scandals. Of all the scandals that have happened, though, one of the most important crises the game has ever faced happened back in 1919. This is a story that involves all of the worst elements of sport – cheating, gambling, and more.

The Black Sox scandal is one of the most damaging moments in the history of the entire sport of baseball. For fans who would have been around in the era, it played a big role in baseball going back the way as a popular sport that the fans loved. A lot of trust was lost in the players, the teams, and the sport itself. Thankfully, baseball recovered and there has not really been a controversy as bad again as the 1919 Black Sox scandal.

The event involved eight members of the Chicago White Sox baseball team. They were accused of giving up and deliberately losing the 1919 World Series against the Cincinnati Reds. The accusation was that in exchange for losing to the Reds, the White Sox players would be given a share of money from a gambling ring that was being run by a man called Arnold Rothstein.

The sport was damaged massively by the scandal, to the point where the National Baseball Commission – who ran the game at the end – was broken down and replaced. The person who replaced the old NBC was a judge, Judge Kenesaw Mountain Landis. Landis was given the position of Commissioner of Baseball, and was given the job of cleaning up the sport and making it respectable once again.

The eight men who were accused of being part of the scandal were all acquitted – allowed to walk away free – from the case in 1921. Landis, though, believed that all of the men should not be allowed to play again, and permanently banned all eight involved from playing professional baseball again. This also ensured that the eight men involved would never be allowed to be considered for the Baseball Hall of Fame. The ban remained for the rest of their professional careers.

The scandal of 1919 was one of the biggest to be found in the history of American sports. It is still seen to this day as one of the worst moments in the history of the sport. Such was the damage done to the league's reputation that many assumed that the league as a whole would never recover from the damage that was done.

Why did the players decide to take part in the scandal? There are believed to be two main reasons. The first reason was quite simple: there was a lot of money involved in the act of deliberately losing. The gambling money would have been a lot more money than many of these players would have made playing baseball professionally. Players in 1919 did not earn the kind of salaries that players earn today; many saw it as a chance to get the kind of money that would set them up for life simply for losing.

However, the other main reason why so many chose to take part was to get back at the owner of the White Sox, Charles Comiskey. Comiskey was not liked by many of the players in the team, and many of the players involved had a special dislike for his attitude towards them.

One of the big names who was involved in the scandal was Joe Jackson. 'Shoeless' Joe Jackson was one of the best players in baseball at the time, and he was seen as the star of the White Sox. He had a great World Series for the White Sox, though, so him admitting that he was involved in the scandal was seen as a huge shock. His teammates, though, said that he was not part of the incident. To this day, nobody knows if he was part of the scheme or if his teammates simply tried to protect one of their most beloved teammates.

The impact of losing so many of their best players, though, killed the White Sox's chances of winning any trophies for the longest time. They would not even have a chance at winning another league pennant until 1936, and they did not win another league championship until 1959. The World Series curse lasted until 2005, meaning that for many the 'Curse of the Black Sox' is the second toughest curse to exist in baseball history after the Curse of the Bambino.

Where did the name come from, though? After all, the players played for the White Sox. Legends claim that the Black Sox name came from the fact that the team was made to pay for washing their own uniforms – something the players refused to do. The players did not do this, and thus their uniforms – once white – became 'black' with dirt and grime from playing the game. The uniforms were eventually washed, though, but the players were made to pay for it out of their own salaries. Some, though, say that this is simply a legend, and the name Black Sox refers to the scandal of the event.

Either way, the Black Sox scandal has gone down in history as one of the worst moments in the history of baseball. The players who were banned tried to save their careers by going on a tour around various parts of the country. However, Judge Landis told any other player who took part in the tour that they would be permanently banned for life as well. The players then intended to play an exhibition match on Sunday afternoons in Chicago, but the city council threatened to cancel any ballpark that allowed the exhibitions to take place.

CHAPTER 4
WHEN JOE NIEKRO WAS CAUGHT RED-HANDED

Baseball is a game of taking risks, and trying to spot opportunities that the other team does not have. Most of the time, this involves some kind of smart tactics or planning. It means that players use every trick in the book to try and come up with ways to get an advantage over the other team. However, it would be fair to say that many players over the years have gone a little bit beyond what is acceptable. Therefore, Major League Baseball is filled with examples of players 'cheating' at the game.

Many players have committed acts that would not be deemed funny. This has often caused them to be banned from the sport. However, those who have taken a more light-hearted approach to gaining an advantage have found themselves becoming part of baseball history. One player who perfectly matches that example is Joe Niekro.

Joe Niekro was a baseball player during the 1960s until the late 1980s. He played for teams like the Chicago Cubs, Detroit Tigers, Houston Astros, New York Yankees, and Minnesota Twins. In his career, he was a one-time All-Star, and also won the World Series in 1987 with the Yankees. In his career, he was a very respected player who was able to produce 1,747 strikeouts in his career. So, he was very good – but he was also known for having an edge to his game. He was known for taking risks.

In 22 years in the game, he enjoyed a great career that saw him become loved by most of the teams that he played for. However, when playing in Minnesota at the end of his career, Niekro was caught 'cheating' in the most hilarious way possible.

Pitching for the Twins in the 1987 season, he was caught taking part in a ball-scuffing incident. As a knuckleball thrower, scuffing the ball could lead to some extra advantages that would make the shot harder to manage for players. In fact, people like the famous umpire Tim Tschida said that Niekro was a 'known ball scuffer' and he seemed to put a lot of gouges in the ball that were much bigger than the usual nicks that a ball gets during the phase of play.

On August 3rd, 1987 Niekro was at the mound for a game against the California Angels. The game is tied at 2-2, going into the fourth inning. As the game progressed, though, Niekro was asked by the umpire for the day, Tschida, to empty his pockets. He emptied his pockets quickly and threw his hands up in the air as if to say "nothing in here, sir!" – however, what came out of his pocket included an emery board and a piece of sandpaper. The board would be used for filing nails, but it could also be used to impact the ball.

Another umpire at the game, Steve Palermo, noticed that the items came out of his pocket as he threw his hands out of his pockets. The objects landed on the ground, and Niekro was asked to explain himself. Niekro said to the umpire that he was simply filing his nails when he was in the dugout waiting to come on. However, the President of the American League at the time, Bobby Brown, did not believe Niekro!

He was then given a 10-day ban by Brown. According to Tschida, though, the trick was actually even more inventive. He claimed in a 2021 interview that Joe Niekro had a piece of sandpaper glued to his hand, and it had been painted to make it look the same colour as his hand. If Niekro wanted to get extra movement on the ball, he would take off his glove and rub the baseball with the sandpaper hand as if he was trying to get a better grip on the ball.

Niekro, though, when asked to empty his pockets, had put his hand in his pocket to try and get the sandpaper to come off his palm. Needless to say, this did not work!

Part of the funny side of the story is the fact that Niekro tries to throw away the emery board file as if nobody is going to notice something flying out of his pocket. His mannerism as he does it, too, - grinning from ear to ear – simply added to the funny nature of the story. While at the time most did see the funny side of it, it was another act that more serious fans saw as an example of the cheating that was so common within baseball at the time.

The Twins did go on to win the game, by the way, winning by a score of 11-3. The ten-day ban, though, was seen as one of the lighter punishments for ball scuffing. All jokes aside, MLB has done a lot over the years to try and bring an end to people scuffing the ball in this way as it is well and truly an act of cheating. However, Niekro was a player who had mostly played fair his whole career outside of ball scuffing, and it was seen as one of the more minor incidents that a player could commit.

The moment of Niekro throwing away the emery board, though, was shown all around the country. Even in a world before social media, the whole baseball world had seen Niekro try to throw away the board. The fact that he was able to walk away while laughing about the incident helped to create a more light-hearted feeling around the whole incident. In fact, while he was suspended, Niekro was invited to go on the "Late Night with David Letterman" TV show, and he turned up wearing a utility belt with a sander on it!

Niekro was known for being a joker and one of the most light-hearted players of his generation in baseball. In fact, when the Twins celebrated their World Series victory, they released a set of bobbleheads in 2017 to mark 30 years since they won the title. Niekro's bobblehead came with a nail file in the back pocket – just like he had that famous day when one of the funniest, and only funny, cheating incidents in MLB took place.

CHAPTER 5
WHEN REGGIE JACKSON BECAME MR. OCTOBER

Ask any older baseball fan in your life, and they will tell you that Reggie Jackson is one of the best baseball players of all-time. When it comes to baseball legends, Reginald Martinez Jackson is one of the all-time heroes. He has achieved everything in the game across a 21-year career in the MLB. He played for various teams, including the Oakland Athletics, the Baltimore Orioles, the New York Yankees, and the California Angels. In his career, he was known for the biggest moments.

Given that the playoffs begin in the latter half of the year in baseball, he became known as 'Mr. October' by many fans due to the fact he would always turn up in the biggest moments. A Baseball Hall of Fame presence, he is regarded as one of the best players of all-time within the league. His ability to keep making hits in the biggest games was a big reason why he won three World Series from 1972 to 1974 with Oakland.

In his career, though, he managed to also win titles with the Yankees, winning the World Series in 1977 and 1978. His career is filled with legendary games and big moments – but no moment can stand taller in his career than his 1977 World Series game six. What happened? Let's find out.

From 1967 until 1987, Jackson played in the league for various teams – his best years came during his first spell with the Kansas City (or Oakland) Athletics, and then a five-year spell with the New York Yankees. A 14-time All-Star, Jackson was on every All-Star team from 1977 until 1984. He won the World Series five times in his career, and was named the MVP of the World Series twice – in 1973 and then 1977. His 1977 performance, though, has gone down in baseball history as one of the most impressive games ever played by any individual.

The 1977 World Series was an interesting one. The Yankees had been the best team in baseball for many years, but they were reaching 15 years since they had last won the World Series. This was a huge drought for a team that had become so used to winning ever since they hired Babe Ruth from the Boston Red Sox. In 1977, then, Jackson arrived as part of a Yankees team that really had to win a World Series once again to restore their name as the biggest team in baseball.

However, things were tough for the Yankees in the early part of the season. Things seemed to get off to a bad start, but as the regular season wore on the Yankees started to find some consistency. In 1977, they managed to go a very impressive 100-62 in the regular season. This was enough to secure their place at the top of the table, and they found themselves back in the World Series. They would face the Los Angeles Dodgers, one of their biggest rivals aside from the Red Sox.

The Yankees enjoyed a tough series, but came to the sixth game of the series 3-2 up against the Dodgers. On October 18th, then, fans were about to see something so impressive that arguably no other player could match or hope to say they had matched. On the night of October 18th, then, the Yankees faced off against the Dodgers knowing that a victory would end their title drought and bring home yet another World Series.

Jackson had been one of the best players in the whole series up to this point, but his performance in the sixth game is arguably one of the best World Series performances ever seen. In the game, he took just one swing each at bat and managed to hit a home run on each of his swings. This kind of success was pretty much impossible to imagine: a player hitting three home runs from only three bats?

It was the stuff of fairytales, and it set the Yankees on a run that saw them win the game 8-4 and thus claim the World Series once again. Jackson's three home runs went down in history as one of the most clutch games of all-time, helping his team to win the game, the series, and the World Series title as a whole. He was named the MVP of the World Series, with his legendary performance making sure that he would always be remembered by Yankees fans as one of the truly best players to ever wear the uniform. To hit three home runs is amazing – to do it from three hits is simply the stuff of dreams.

After this amazing performance, Jackson was dubbed 'Mr. October' by the media and by Yankees fans. In yet another major series in October, Jackson had turned up and played the game to the very best of his ability. And what ability he had. This only cemented his position as one of the truly best players to ever play the game – and throughout his career, it was always referenced as his crowning moment.

Later in his career, Jackson also served as an advisor to the Houston Astros. In 2022, the Astros went on to win the World Series, so fans could argue that Jackson played a big part in getting the Astros over the line. Though he did not play or coach the Astros, it is believed that his input and his experience was a big part of the team going all the way to win the title.

Even nearly forty years after stopping playing, Reggie Jackson is still having an impact on the sport. There is a reason why your older family members will talk about him with so much love: Reggie Jackson is, for many, the best player of their younger years. He was and is one of the greatest ever baseball players to ever pick up a bat, and he is seen by many as the finest example of long-term success.

Since making his debut in 1967 to his impact on the 2022 Astros, then, Jackson Is one of the best of all-time. His 1977 performance, though, will definitely go down in history as one of the greatest stories ever told in baseball.

CHAPTER 6
THE CURSE OF THE BAMBINO

Professional baseball is filled with many stories that sound like they come from a storybook. While the support itself can be rather slow-paced, baseball has a habit of creating stories that are as exciting off the field as they are on. One of the most famous stories in all of baseball history is the story of Babe Ruth. If you have never heard of Babe Ruth, then you might never have heard of the Curse of the Bambino. This is one of the most infamous events to ever take place within Major League Baseball (MLB).

As any baseball fan knows, the Boston Red Sox and the New York Yankees are arguably the two biggest names in the league. They have a worldwide fan base, and they are some of the most recognized names in all sports. Like most Boston and New York sports teams, there is an intense rivalry between the two sides. A big part of that rivalry came from the story that we are about today. It is about a man named Babe Ruth – arguably the best baseball player of all-time.

The early years of MLB saw the Red Sox emerge as by far and away the dominant team within the league. In the first fifteen seasons of MLB, the Red Sox were the champions five times. They won the first-ever World Series in 1903 and became the most impressive side in the league. A big part of this early success came from being ahead of other teams when it came to finding the best players.

Among the very best was Ruth. He started his career playing in the minor leagues, including for the Baltimore Orioles. His incredible performances made the Red Sox become interested, and he joined them in 1914. He joined the team in July of that year, alongside Ernie Shore and Ben Egan. The trio came to Boston, and they won their first game as Red Sox players, winning 4-3 against the Cleveland Naps.

His impact on the team was instant. As a starting pitcher, he was incredible for the Red Sox. He was a key part in early success. Despite being a top-class pitcher, Ruth decided to make the change to the role of an outfielder. On days when Ruth would not be pitching, he would play outfield instead. This change helped the team to continually win trophies during his four-year spell as part of the Red Sox.

His arrival as part of the Red Sox began another run of trophies. Ruth was a crucial part of the Red Sox, being a dominant team in the 1910s. He helped them to win the World Series three times – in 1915, 1916, and then 1918. With the team so successful, you would think that they would keep on winning, right?

That they would keep a winning team together? No!

Boston reached a bad spot after winning in 1918. In 1919, they finished in sixth place – a disaster for a team that was so used to lifting trophies. Boston decided that it was time to move on from their star player. His behavior off the field – regularly smoking, drinking, and fighting – had led to the ball club looking for reasons to move on for good. In 1919, then, the Red Sox decided that it was time to get rid of "Bambino" himself – and they traded him, as well as most of their other "star" players, for new players.

When trading Ruth, though, the owner of the Red Sox at the time, Harry Frazee, needed money to help fund a Broadway show he was producing. So, in trading Ruth, he did not look for players back in return. Instead, he asked for $100,000 in cash to be sent to Boston. Not a single player was traded for Ruth – only money. Trading him to the unsuccessful Yankees seemed like a great idea, too: what would Ruth be able to achieve in such a lowly team?

For Boston, the reality was that they had just traded away arguably the greatest baseball player of all-time. They traded Ruth to the Yankees, and in a short space of time they became the most dominant team in the entire MLB. They have since won more than double the number of World Series titles as any other MLB team – including, of course, the Red Sox.

A rivalry soon formed between the two teams. The "Curse of the Bambino" was formed, as Boston would not win another title until the 2004 World Series. Interestingly, though, the actual "Curse of the Bambino" name did not become commonly used until 1990. After that, though, the name stuck and lasted for close to 15 years before the Red Sox finally ended their own heartbreak.

However, while Ruth was the main factor in the "Curse" becoming a thing, other reasons exist. For example, Babe Ruth was joined at the Yankees by the General Manager of the Red Sox, Ed Barrow, as well as other key players in their title success of the 1910s.

The curse seemed to stick around for well over 80 years, with the Boston team suffering "cursed" defeats several times over the years to come. For example, the Red Sox reached their first World Series since the sale of Babe Ruth in 1946. They played the St. Louis Cardinals and were expected to win easily. However, they threw the game away and lost the title to the Cardinals.

Other examples include the 1967 season, when they lost again to the Cardinals in a 7-game series. Other World Series losses in that time include losses to the Cincinnati Reds in 1975, and the New York Mets in 1986.

While the curse today has finally been broken once and for all, the "Curse of the Bambino" is one of the most famous stories in sports history. The mistake of creating a rivalry with the Yankees, now the most successful team in baseball, is one thing. Trading to them the player who went on to make the Yankees as popular and as successful as they are today will go down as the biggest mistake in the history of American sports!

CHAPTER 7
THE CURSE OF THE BAMBINO IS BROKEN

Baseball is a sport that is filled with exciting stories. Of teams making one single move that can make or break their season. For some teams, though, a single move can mean more than just one season of glory or failure. For the Boston Red Sox, trading Babe Ruth in 1918 set in motion a series of events that would see them fail to win another World Series title for close to 90 years!

The Boston Red Sox are one of the biggest sports teams in America. They are known all around the world, too, for being arguably the next biggest Major League Baseball team after the New York Yankees. However, without their own mistakes, the Red Sox might be the de facto super team of the MLB. Instead, a 1918 trade to the Yankees sent Ruth to a team that, up to that point, had done very little in the league.

After the arrival of Ruth, though, the Yankees went on to become the most important team in the MLB. At the time of writing, the Yankees have twenty seven World Series titles – more than double the next team. Next on the list of winners is the St. Louis Cardinals, with 11, and then the Oakland Athletics with 9 World Series wins. The Boston Red Sox also have 9, and boast the best winning percentage in World Series finals – they have won 9 while losing only 4. The Yankees, meanwhile, have won 27 whilst losing 13.

They are by far and away the biggest team in baseball, and it is all down to trading for Ruth for cash considerations back in the day. This set the Yankees on a series of title wins – from 1921 until 1928 they won 6 of their 27 titles. Five years with the Red Sox seen Ruth win three World Series titles; with the Yankees, though, he won another 4 titles – 1923, 1927, 1928, and 1932.

Without him, the Yankees probably never become the force they are today. With Ruth, the Red Sox probably continue to be the biggest team in baseball and would likely have never fallen by the wayside. Instead, what happened with the trade was that Boston did not win another title until 2004. For many of you dear readers, that was probably before you were even born!

The experience that led to the Red Sox suffering from the Curse of the Bambino was hard to fathom. They lost numerous World Series titles in that time, including losing the 1946 World Series – their first since Ruth left – as well as losing the 1967 World Series to the Cardinals. They also lost the title in 1975, losing to the Cincinnati Reds. Other World Series losses came in 1986 – losing to the New York Mets.

They also suffered many close run things, such as missing out on the chance to take part in the World Series. This included missing out on the World Series in 1948, 1949, 1978, 1988, 1990 and 2003. So, for long-suffering fans of the Red Sox, the team has gone through decades of pain and hurt.

Despairing fans tried all manner of things to try and break the curse. For example, a fan placed a Red Sox cap atop Mount Everest, burning a Yankees cap at base camp. One famous example came in 1976, when Massachusetts' 'Official Witch', Laurie Cabot, was brought in to end the curse. The Red Sox were on a 10-game losing run; while the losses stopped, the World Series wait did not.

Other ridiculous ideas were suggested, too. For example, in 1994, the Red Sox pitcher, Bill Lee, recommended that the Red Sox exhumed Ruth's body – he died after the Second World War – and bring it back to Fenway Park, the home of the Red Sox, so they could apologise for trading him. Needless to say, that did not happen!

In 2004, though, it would all finally change. The curse would come to an end in one of the most famous moments in all of baseball history. Fittingly, the Red Sox had to face off against the Yankees in the American League Championship. Despite losing the first three games of the series – including a 19-8 defeat in the third game – the Red Sox rallied.

They tied the game thanks to a stolen base by Dave Roberts, and won the match on a two-run home run thanks to David Ortiz. The Red Sox, then, came back to win the series after winning the next three games. In doing so, they managed to be the first team ever – and so far only – in MLB to win a seven-game series once they have lost the first three games. Surely, now, the curse was set to be broken?!

The Red Sox would face off against another big team in the World Series: the St. Louis Cardinals. Having already lost to them in 1946 and then 1967, it was a bit of history repeating itself. Third time lucky, right?

For the Red Sox, though, the hard work had been done in the previous games with the Yankees. Beating the old enemy in such a special way was enough to give the team the spirit and confidence they needed. They managed to beat the Cardinals with ease, winning the series in a four-game streak. The Red Sox won the first three games with ease, and in Game 4, on October 27th 2004, they took on the Cardinals one more time.

86 years of hurt came to an end that night, and one of the biggest teams in baseball managed to finally break the unique curse. Some fans say that the curse itself was broken in September, not October, of 2004. Why? Because of a very special moment. Manny Ramirez hit a ball into the stands, and it was attempted to be caught by Lee Gavin, a 16-year-old fan of the team. Gavin lived on a farmhouse in Sudbury, Massachusetts – the same farmhouse where Ruth himself had grown up!

While Gavin missed the catch and lost his two front teeth, many say that on his way to hospital in the ambulance he took the curse with him. And so, the curse was broken – one way or another, the Boston Red Sox won the 2004 World Series with ease. And with it, one of the most unique losing runs in the history of American sports came to an end.

Will there ever be another curse quite like The Curse of the Bambino? It is unlikely. For fans of the Red Sox, and of baseball, though, this is one of the most unique stories in the history of the sport.

CHAPTER 8
THE BREAKING OF THE MLB COLOR BARRIER

Major League Baseball is a league that is famous for its heroes. While every sport has its legends, baseball more than most is built on the work of these superstars. Most baseball legends are known for home runs, amazing hits, or super catches. Others, though, are known for changing the way the game is watched.

One of the most important people in the history of MLB, then, is Jackie Robinson. If you have never heard of Jackie, then you are about to find out about a true baseball legend. Here is the story of one of the most important moments in the history of MLB – and it was brought about by Jackie Robinson himself.

The league has changed time and time again across its 100-plus years of service. Fans have seen the game change not only in how it is played, but also who plays the game. For example, did you know that once upon a time white and black players were not allowed to play on the same team? This shameful episode was a big part of baseball in America for a large portion of its early life as a sport in the country.

Out of all of the events that have happened in MLB, it would be hard to find an event more important to the development of the game than Jackie Robinson's appearance as a player. Once upon a time, then, players of different skin colors were not allowed to be part of the same team – or the same league. Instead, black players would play in a different league while white players were allowed to play in MLB.

That was a terrible decision, but thankfully Jackie and others came along to change the history of baseball forever. In 1947, Jackie Robinson was signed by the Brooklyn Dodgers and made his debut that year. In doing so, he became the first black player to play in the MLB. This was in 1947, around eight years before the all-important Civil Rights Movement.

His debut with the Dodgers was a major moment for the league. A hugely impressive 26,623 fans turned up to watch the game that night – and as many as 14,000 were black baseball supporters. At first, Robinson was given more than a small amount of abuse from the crowd. He found it hard to settle, and he felt doubts as to whether or not he should stick around. Was he causing more trouble than it was worth? Would it be better to just go back to the old leagues he played in?

Luckily, two people on the team had a different idea. Coach Leo Durocher and teammate Pee Wee Reese stood up for Robinson against the racism he faced. They defended him, spoke up for his ability as a player and his quality as a person, and made sure that he was accepted and welcomed by fans and players alike. He was accepted by his own club – but that was not the end of this sad, but important, story.

Other teams in the league were less willing to accept playing against a non-white player. For example, when the Dodgers went to play the St. Louis Cardinals, players on the opposition team considered holding a protest. They wanted to make clear that, in their eyes, having non-white players in the league was not allowed.

The Cardinals were not the only team who held such horrible views, sadly. Other people who held such opinions included the Philadelphia Phillies. Their players were very outspoken about the fact that Robinson would be playing, and were clear that they did not want to share the field with him. Legends of the time say that the Dodgers team were so upset about what was being said about Robinson that they wanted to stand by him even more. Every player on the team, even those who were not sure at first, now backed Robinson 100% to be part of the Dodgers team.

After his debut in the league, though, eyes were opened to just how much talent was being left out of the league. Other teams started to look at black players, too, and more and more teams started to see the idea of signing a black player as something that they should be doing. The other first black players to come into the league included the likes of Satchel Paige, Don Newcombe, Roy Campanella, and Larry Doby. All four of these men found success in the league, and before long any racial tensions within the league started to fade away. The players and coaches were happy with the new arrangement, and so the fans would need to also accept that this was the new way of doing things.

The success that Robinson brought on the field was another big reason why so many realized they were wrong. Robinson was a major part of the 1955 Dodgers World Series win, helping them to win the title. In doing so, he set the stall for himself to become a World Series champion and a future Hall of Famer. Not only did Robinson help to open the door to racial equality within the league, but he helped to remove the stigma that existed about black players being part of the MLB.

His impact on the game was huge, and it is believed that the multiracial nature of MLB in the years to come played a major role in the eventual Civil Rights Movement taking place. Though Robinson and others took a lot of abuse in their early days in the league, they persevered. They stuck it out. They waited.

When it comes to big events in the history of baseball, Jackie Robinson making his debut as the first black man to play in the MLB is one of the most important ever. Not only did it have a huge impact on the sport of baseball, but it played a big role in convincing other parts of society to change their tune. America became a better place thanks to the efforts of Robinson and his Dodgers teammates to show the world that, regardless of skin color, all who could play baseball were welcome in the major leagues.

CHAPTER 9
GAME 7 OF THE 2016 WORLD SERIES

Some baseball seasons are more memorable than others. Most of the time, it comes down to who wins the title and how the title is won. For most fans of the sport, though, there will always be a personal favourite season; a season that stands out more than any other for how downright unique it was. For fans of the Chicago Cubs, the highlight series of all-time might very well be the 2016 World Series.

The Cubs would go on to play the Cleveland Indians in the World Series, with the Cubs winning the National League and the Indians winning the American League. Both teams would go ahead and meet in the World Series itself, the first time they had ever faced-off against one another in the history of the post-season. For fans up and down the country, and across the world, the showpiece 2016 event is one of the most exciting of all-time.

With the exception of the years 1919-1921, all World Series title games are best-of-seven playoff tournaments that see the two champions of the respective leagues face off against one another. The games took place between the 25th October and the 2nd November – though the final game, Game 7, ran past midnight and thus technically ended on the 3rd November.

This was the last World Series to determine the home court advantage team based on who won the All Star match-up. The American League had won the All-Star game this year, so the Indians were given home-court advantage. Speak to baseball fans in your family, and you will find that the 2016 World Series is considered one of the greatest baseball stories of all-time. Why?

For one, both teams were romantic stories – neither were really expected to get anywhere near the World Series at the start of the year. Even as they both showed impressive form during the season, nobody really counted either team as a legitimate title winner. Most times, a World Series will have a favourite and an underdog; this was different. The two teams both came into the series with the intention of retaining that underdog status – nobody wanted to be the favourite!

Another big reason why this series is so beloved by fans of the game is that it was so competitive. Each game was really quite fun to watch for fans – they were all very tight games. Most World Series events will feature at least one major blowout victory – this was not the case here at all. Instead, it was one of the tightest series ever seen in MLB.

While the whole series was a lot of fun for fans to watch, the seventh game of the series is regarded as one of the best games of all-time in the league. The seventh game was only the fifth World Series seventh game to go into extra innings – and it was the first for close to 20 years, with the last being in 1997. Interestingly, it was also the first Game 7 in history to have a rain delay to stop the game at around the 10th inning.

Let us paint the picture. The Cubs were down 3-1 after four matches of the series, and it looked like the Indians were going to keep the Cubs down. The Cubs are a massive name in American baseball, having played in 11 World Series titles. However, this was their first appearance in the Series since 1945, and it was also their chance to win their first title since 1908. If they were to win, it would be their third title – and it would end the longest wait for a world title in North American sports.

The Indians, meanwhile, had been in six World Series events, though none since 1997, and they had not won the title since 1948 either. So, for fans of the sport, it was a chance to see a name on the cup who had not won the title for a long time. Given that both teams were among the two with the longest waits for a World Series win – over 176 seasons combined without winning! – this was a special occasion for fans of the sport. It was also the chance to see two great fanbases finally have a shot at winning the World Series.

Game 7, though, will go down as one of the most special games to ever be played in any baseball stadium. The game went on for a long time, with many saying that it was the greatest Game 7 ever. The game was tense and there was plenty of back and forth, but as the game went into the extra innings it was the Cubs who looked like they were going to be able to take control.

In the crowds at the Wrigley Field stadium was Bill Murray, one of the most devoted Cubs fans there ever will be. The comedian watched on as his team finally took control, and when Mike Montgomery – who had no career saves in his history – retired Michael Martinez, the game was over. The Cubs won the Championship for the first time in all of those years!

A 108-year trophy drought came to an end, and they were able to finally show off the trophy that every Chicago sports fan had wanted the most. Chicago sports fans had seen the likes of the Chicago Bulls win the NBA trophy several times in the 1990s. But you would need to be very lucky indeed to have seen the Cubs last World Series win.

As such, the celebrations went long into the night. Most fans argue to this day that the rain delay is the main reason why the Cubs went on to win. The delay gave them a chance to regroup when it looked like the Indians were going to take full control. The Cubs also became the first team to come back from 3-1 down to win a World Series since the 1985 Kansas City Royals.

History was made that night, and it ensured that the Cubs could finally stop being seen as a 'cursed' sports team in America. They also passed on their 'curse' to the Indians, who now became the proud owners of the longest championship drought in the league – currently at 74 years.

For Chicago sports fans, this is one of the most famous moments in their history. Being able to win the game in such a unique way – and using the rain delay, the first ever in a Game 7, to their advantage – only further helped to ensure that the 2016 World Series went down as an all-time classic.

CHAPTER 10
THE INSECT INVASION OF OCTOBER 5TH 2007

As one of the most exciting leagues in the world, Major League Baseball has produced some stories that will never be forgotten. Most of these stories involve players or clubs doing something amazing. Sometimes, though, the story comes to life due to nature itself. One of the best examples of this can be found on October 5th, 2007.

The game was an important match for the Cleveland Indians and the New York Yankees. Both teams were playing each other in the American League Division Series, and the stakes were high. Both teams were eager to win, but nobody could have imagined what would get in the way of success in this match.

On the October 5th match-up between the Indians and the Yankees, the Yankees were expected to win against an Indians team that had been very successful ever since they came into the league in 1994. The Indians had won the division title in 2007, with a record of 96-66. They would therefore face the Yankees, who had finished with a 94-68 record.

The Yankees had gone 6-0 in the regular season against the Indians, so they were very confident that they could out the other side of this and win. The Indians had been a successful team during their first 13 or so years in the league, but the Yankees are – and were – still the

Yankees. New York had been part of the post-season every year since 1995, having won four World Series triumphs since 1995, meaning they were the most successful team of the modern era.

However, in the first game of this ALDS series, the Indians destroyed the Yankees by a score of 12-3. The second game of the series was to begin at 5.07PM in Cleveland, and the Yankees manager, Joe Torre, put forward Andy Pettitte to the hill. Up against him was Fausto Carmona. Carmona had enjoyed a great season in 2007, and was one of the most important players on this particular Cleveland team.

Thanks to the warm weather and the fact that the lights of the stadium were so vivid, though, a unique thing happened: a small army of midges appeared!

The midges were brought to the stadium simply due to the heat and due to the existence of the massive light systems. With the Yankees 1-0 up going into the bottom of the eighth, the midges turned up and took over the entire park. Swarms of them came around the pitcher's mound, and one player in particular seemed to get the worst of it: Joba Chamberlain.

The images of that day are still some of the most unique ever seen in baseball today. There was a swarm all around the pitcher's mound, and Chamberlain himself was covered all around his neck and arms with midges. He asked for bug spray to see if that would help to repel the midges, but it did nothing to really help at all. Chamberlain said, with no shortage of irony, that "they bugged me" – but he tried to play on.

The bugs hung around for about 45 minutes, and had a big impact on the match. It impacted on the concentration of the players who were batting, and it stopped the game from having any real flow for much of those 45 minutes. In the end, the Indians went on to win the game, defeating the Yankees in four games. The Indians would go on to play the Boston Red Sox. Going 3-1 up before losing and seeing Boston go to the World Series once again.

For the Yankees, though, success would not be far away: they won the World Series once again in 2009. No matter what, though, this game would always be remembered as one of the strangest in all of MLB history. Bugs have appeared before at games, but the sheer amount of bugs was like something that had never been seen before.

Chamberlain admitted that he felt that he could not even open his mouth because he was scared of swallowing some of these critters. It was believed that an unseasonal warmth of around 81 degrees at first pitch meant that the bugs were naturally attracted to the heat that was in the air. With the lights being on, too, it was another reason why they bugs decided to appear at such staggering numbers.

Chamberlain also said that it "ain't normal" for bugs to be so close to the pitch. Given that this match is one of the most famous in MLB history due to the bugs, it would be fair to say that he is right. Despite using a canister of bug spray – that later went on auction as part of sports history – the bugs would not move until later on in the match.

Yankees manager Joe Torre has since admitted that he should have taken his team off the field. Given that it likely stopped the Yankees from winning on the night, it is easy to see why he might feel that way!

Though the memory is one that Yankees fans will always remember, the fact it cost them a chance to go to the World Series again was a big blow to the team. It stopped their progress and meant that it was another season of "failure" after so many years of success in the years before.

Still, for MLB fans, the "bug game" is one of the most famous in the league's history. Given that it has never happened before or since, it stands out as one of the most unique moments to ever happen in the whole of the MLB.

CHAPTER 11
HARVEY HADDIX NEARLY HITS THE PERFECT GAME

The perfect game. For many players, it is something they never get close to achieving in their careers. In fact, for most. It is one of the hardest things to do in professional baseball. The list of players who have completed a perfect game is tiny. Many, though, have come very close to this achievement. Close, though, is not enough!

One player who came very close to achieving the perfect game was Harvey Haddix. Harvey Haddix was born on September 18th, 1925, and enjoyed a very good career in the baseball world. He played for teams like the St. Louis Cardinals, Philadelphia Phillies, Cincinnati Redlegs, Pittsburgh Pirates, and Baltimore Orioles. He is probably best known for his time with the Cardinals, but it was with the Pirates that he nearly pulled off the most remarkable feat that a baseball player can achieve.

The night was May 26th, 1959, and he was playing amazingly well. Haddix was an excellent player, but he was not a superstar: while he was always liked by the teams he played for, and their fans, he was not seen as a star by any kind of metric. However, his form that year had been good – he was playing for the Pirates, and the May 26th game was the ideal chance to show the fans what he could do.

The Pirates were playing the Milwaukee Braves, in Milwaukee, at the Milwaukee County Stadium. Haddix started the game well, and continued to hit very impressive form as the game went on. It was early in the season, so nobody was expecting someone to be pitching so well – but by the 12th inning, Haddix was still having a perfect game. This was no surprise in some ways, though; he was a three-time All-Star and respected across the league as a batter of high quality.

However, even the best pitchers in baseball struggle to go as long as Haddix was on the 26th May. He kept hitting through everything, and the fact it was against the Braves, who had been to the World Series in each of the last two years, was even more impressive. Haddix was playing a fine game – he was in total control, and had managed to retire as many as 27 different Braves across the first nine innings of the game.

Interestingly, though, the game was still tied at 0-0 after nine innings. Lew Burdette of the Braves was having a fine game himself, and had kept the score at zero zero. Haddix came back to the mound for the next three innings, though, and in that time he managed to retire the nine Braves that he faced off against – 36 up, 36 down, and a truly remarkable run of form that was never really expected of any player.

However, Felix Mantilla came to the 13th inning and he hit an easy shot to third base. However, the throw had managed to pull Haddix off-base, and thus the perfect game came to an abrupt end. He was replaced by teammate Joe Adcock, who managed to hit a home run. However, things did not work out on the day: Mantilla managed to pull off a run, the league ruled that it counted, while the other runs did not, and thus the Braves were given a 1-0 win by the National League.

Haddix managed to retire 36 straight batters, which has something that has never been done before or since. It is a strange story, then, to imagine that maybe the greatest ever pitched game in the history of Major League Baseball ended up in a 1-0 defeat on a run that was arguably never earned.

For Haddix, though, this was the kind of ill luck that would plague certain parts of his career. Missing out on the chance to have one of the most impressive runs of all-time ruined by such ill fortune was a huge blow for Haddix and for his teammates. The game, though, went down in history as one of the strangest ever to be played within the league. All of these years later, it is still remembered as one of base-ball's most unique sporting moments.

Indeed, a banquet was held in 1989 by players from both teams who wanted to talk about one of the greatest MLB moments of their playing careers. For Haddix, though, being able to strike out so many batters from such a high level team was a huge achievement. It was the kind of achievement that is remembered forever, even if the actual result of the game did not go the way that the Pirates had wanted.

In fact, even to this day it is considered by many within the league to be the best pitching performance in the history of the major leagues. While it might not have ended the way that Haddix would have wanted, he is still remembered all of these years later for nearly achieving something that is almost impossible to replicate. For many baseball fans, it is one of the most remarkable achievements – even if it did not result in a win, Haddix did manage to take out as many as 36 different opponents in a single evening.

Sadly for Haddix, the league changed the regulations around what a no-hitter is in 1991, and his record was taken away from him. Haddix, though, admitted that "I know what I did" later on in his life. Despite the record being taken away from the actual record books, fans of baseball will always remember May 26th, 1959, as the day that Harvey Haddix nearly completed the rarest of things: the perfect game.

Perfect games are so rare because they are so hard: the difficulty is proven by the fact that all of these years later we still remember a player coming as close as Haddix did to achieving it. If he had achieved the perfect game, then it would no doubt have gone down in history as the most impressive pitching performance ever seen within the history of MLB.

CHAPTER 12
WHEN PETE ROSE PASSED TY COBB

Baseball records are, in the main, made to be broken. Like every sporting record, there is an expectation that one day someone will break that record. Someone will do the same thing, but only better. However, some records feel like they are never going to be broken – and in the case of Pete Rose, becoming the all-time 'hit king' was a truly special moment in his career.

The record that he broke belonged to Ty Cobb, and at the time of the record being broken it had stood for close to 60 years. The record? To be the number one all-time player to hit singles in their career. The record set by Ty Cobb was an amazing improvement, because the previous holder, Eddie Collins, had around 2,643 singles in his career. Cobb managed to break the 3,000 mark, achieving 3,053 singles in his career. The record stood for 57 years in total, before the legendary Pete Rose came along and broke the record once and for all.

Nobody has gotten close to breaking the record since it was set – in fact, only the two players mentioned – Rose and Cobb – have broken the 3,000 mark when it comes to career singles. Given how important a single is in baseball, it is a huge surprise that nobody has even come close to breaking the mark.

A single is very important in the game of baseball, and it is the most common type of hit delivered by a batter. Basically, a single is a batter getting to first base by hitting the ball – becoming a runner in doing so – and getting to first base before they are put out by an opposition fielder. Singles, then, are very important to progressing in the game of baseball, and they are one of the most common actions seen on the pitch.

Pete Rose was, during his career, considered one of the best in Major League Baseball. He was a great hitter of the ball, and he played for teams like the Cincinnati Reds. During his time with the Reds, he was known as part of The Big Red Machine; one of the best line-ups in baseball at the time. They dominated the National League during the 1970s, and Rose was a major part of that team. Rose also played for teams like the Philadelphia Phillies and the Montreal Expos, but his main career success came as part of the Reds.

Across his career, he achieved many great records as a player. For example, he is the all-time leader in baseball when it comes to hits – hitting 4,256 – as well as games played, at 3,562. He also is the career leader in outs, with 10,328. His career record of singles, though, is one of the most impressive of all of his records. In his career, he won the World Series three times, and was also the Most Valuable Player award winner once. He played as an All-Star 17 times, and played a total of 23 years in the MLB.

He also played five different positions in All-Star games, a feat that has also stood as an unbroken record since he achieved it. A Golden Glove winner in 1969 and 1970, too, his career was full of amazing achievements. It was his achievement in 1984, though, that set him apart from the rest of the class. At the time, Rose was the player-manager of the Reds, and was the tender age of 44.

Rose was someone who loved to be able to set and break records, and it was his immense skill and versatility that made him such a beloved player by fans of all teams. His chance to go and break such a special record was something that seemed almost impossible at the time. Fans of the game believed that Cobb's records would never be broken, and the fact that it had stood during the Deadball Era of the game meant that many believed no player in the Modern Era of the game would have a chance at breaking such a record.

However, with Rose, he valued being able to simply keep the ball in play as opposed to the excessive power that many sluggers used of the time. He was able to hit his 3,215 singles simply by being very consistent and always doing his best to keep the ball in the game and move to first base. Breaking that record in 1984, then, was seen as one of the most impressive moments of what was already a very impressive career.

On the 11th September, 1985, he took to the field against San Diego and would have the chance of breaking a 57-year-old record set by Ty Cobb – only this time it was for hits. The game proceeded as planned, and during the first inning he lined a single to the left-center for his 4,192nd hit. This broke the record of Ty Cobb that day to become the all-time hitter in the league – one of the most impressive records seen in the whole of MLB.

His career continued for a while longer, though, and he managed to get another 64 hits in total meaning that he ended up with a career total of 4,256 hits. That is a number that is unlikely to be broken given the way that the game is played today. Therefore, while many thought that Cobb's record would never be stopped or beaten, most now say the same about Rose's record.

Rose's career in baseball was all about breaking records and being an all-timer, but he did have some issues in the game as well. For example, in 1989, Rose was banned from the sport after allegations that he had been gambling on baseball when he should not have been. An investigation was held by the league, and Rose said that he was not involved in any gambling.

However, while at first the case was dropped, he was eventually banned by the league after being accused of betting on the game during the years of 1985 and 1987. He denied the accusation quite seriously, but he was given a voluntary banishment from the sport for a year. It was a major black mark on what was once one of the all-time great records.

The betting issue aside, though, nobody can take away the success and the great form that Rose achieved during his career. He was able to become a career leader in so many different stats, which surely stands for more than a betting mistake made later in life.

CHAPTER 13

THE FIRST EVER MAJOR LEAGUE BASEBALL ALL-STAR GAME

For fans of all the major American sports, the All-Star game is something that fans from all around the country love to watch. The All-Star game is for the fans: the chance to see dream team style line-ups of players at the highest level. However, while it has been a major part of each of the big American sports for years now, the All-Star game was not always something that was played. In fact, for Major League Baseball, the first All-Star game did not take place for quite some time.

The first ever edition of the All-Star game, then, took place in the 1933 season. It was decided that something should be held during the midsummer to help give fans the chance to see the best players in the league competing alongside one another. The game was decided to take place between the National League and American League, with each league choosing the best players from across each team to take part. This, then, was the beginning of a new tradition that has stuck to this day.

The very first All-Star exhibition took place on July 6th, 1933, and it was held at Comiskey Park. It was part of the Chicago World's Fair that was part of the city's celebrations. The idea was first brought to the table by Arch Ward, a member of the newspaper The Chicago Tribune. He had been approached by the Mayor of Chicago at the time,

Edward J. Kelly, about holding a major sports event as part of the World's Fair.

The game was held during what was known as the Great Depression, a time of real hardship for many in the country. It was hoped that such a big-name exhibition match would help to raise the mood of the local people. Fans would vote to pick a starting line-up of nine players, while the managers would choose the other nine, and the players would all come from the National League and American League respectively.

It was dubbed the "Game of the Century" by the Tribune, and ballots were printed in the newspapers of America so that fans would get the chance to vote for the players they wanted to see in this big showpiece event. The game, then, was held on the 6th July and it was attended by just under 50,000 people. Around $45,000 was raised, a lot of money at the time, and it went towards both charitable events and players in the league who were in need of financial help.

The game itself was a huge success, with Babe Ruth of the New York Yankees hitting a two-run home run in the third inning. He also caught a fly ball right next to the scoreboard in the eighth inning. It was a truly showpiece exhibition game, with fans from all over the country coming to watch what was a huge event. Many legends of the era played in the game, including the famous Lou Gehrig.

In fact, twenty of the players who played out of the thirty six in total were later added to the Baseball Hall of Fame. This just goes to show the high level of baseball that was being played on the day. The same went for the coaches: the two game managers, and five of the six coaches involved, would be added into the Hall of Fame themselves. Even two of the four umpires eventually joined the Hall of Fame!

The game itself was a fun experience, with the American League team eventually winning the day after a lot of hard fought challenges. Many big names of the day played, with the likes of Babe Ruth and Lefty Gomez playing in the game. Ruth, then, held the record of being the first baseball player to score a home run within the All-Star game.

The reasons for holding the All-Star game were quite varied, but from 1930 to 1933 the baseball league had seen attendances drop quite a lot. Indeed, attendances had dropped by as much as 40%, while the salary of players had dropped by around one quarter due to the lack of fans turning up. Tickets were too expensive due to the Great Depression, and so fans had to pick and choose what they could spend their money on. This led to money falling out of the league, and salaries being slashed for all.

The need to find ways to make the game more modern and more exciting became a common talking point. The idea of using something like an All-Star game was floated, and it was hoped that this would get more fans back in the door as well as give some extra money to the players who were finding it hard to make ends meet due to the cuts happening to their salaries.

Ever since it was first brought to the table, though, the All-Star game has taken place every single year apart from two years: 1945, and 2020. For 1945, the All-Star game did not happen due to the Second World War, while the 2020 edition did not take place due to the COVID-19 pandemic. Other than this, though, the All-Star game has been an annual moment to savour for fans up and down the country – and across the world.

What was supposed to be a one-off "Game of the Century", then, became an annual part of baseball that will always be part of US sports. The All-Star game is one of the best days on the calendar for fans of any of the major sports. Getting to see the very best in the sport line up together in different dream team combinations has always been something that fans have found exciting. The fact that there is such a love for the All-Star game long after it was first introduced goes to show what a great idea it was.

Even with various adjustments and changes over the years, what makes the All-Star game so great still remains to this day. For fans of the sport, tuning in to watch the All-Star game is a privilege in itself.

CHAPTER 14
THE STORY OF THE ST. LOUIS BROWNS

The world of Major League Baseball has always been a pretty competitive sports league. Most of the teams who have been in the league for years have found themselves having at least once season of success. Most teams have had the chance to at least enjoy some kind of trophy success, or reach a World Series. One team that only ever enjoyed one season of success, though, was the St. Louis Browns.

Today, you might know them as the Baltimore Orioles. Before the 1953 season, though, the Orioles played in St. Louis and were known instead as the St. Louis Browns. Interestingly, though, the Browns actually started life in the American League as the Milwaukee Brewers. While the Brewers eventually became a team in their own right, the Browns continued to exist – barely.

The Brewers were first formed in Milwaukee, and played there until the 1901 baseball season when they were moved to St. Louis. There, they became known as the St. Louis Browns and would play 52 years in Missouri. Those years, though, were mostly years of failure. This is the story of the St. Louis Browns one season of success in their entire history.

The Browns are probably known as being the worst team in the history of the MLB in terms of success. For the majority of their 52-year history in Missouri, they enjoyed one season of success: during the Second World War no less. In fact, many jokes have been made over the years that it took a World War for the Browns to find any kind of success!

The 1940s was a period of challenge for the MLB. Many of the best players were shipped away to take part in the war, some going on the front lines. The Second World War became the main topic of conversation in the 1940s, and it meant that many Americans took part in the war in Europe and in Asia in particular. However, for the Browns, this gave them a chance to finally savour some kind of success.

During the War, the fittest and most famous players were asked to take part in the war effort. As such, many of the baseball teams still in America at the time were unable to field their best players. The Browns, though, were usually made up of average players who had tasted no real success on the field, or, they had players who other teams would not accept due to their behaviour. Other players were simply beyond their sell-by date, and were seen as players who would not be beneficial to the war effort.

So, the Browns managed to keep most of their 'best' players during the war as even the army did not want them to be involved. As various superstars left to go and fight in the war, the Browns had the rare opportunity to keep their team together. Now, in comparison to most of the other teams weakened by the war, the Browns were now a decent potential contender for success!

The 1944 season, then, is by far and away the best – and only – real success in the history of the St. Louis Browns. In that season, they finished with a record of 89-65. In most normal seasons that would be nowhere near good enough to get a team close to an American League or National League pennant.

For the Browns, though, this was good enough to secure them the American League pennant for the first time. Even this, though, was a close run thing. The Browns had to win 11 of their last 12 games just to win the pennant by a single game!

Even with so much of an advantage over other teams in the league who had lost their star players, the Browns just about scraped through to the World Series. Their opponent in the World Series would be the St. Louis Cardinals, so it was a bit of a rivalry and a derby for fans to watch. Was this finally the time when the Browns would get a chance to win something and have their day in the spotlight?

As it would turn out, no. The Browns lost in six games to their city rivals. They lost most of the games quite comfortably, too, with the players involved simply not capable of handling the stress of being in the World Series. The Browns strategy of picking up players who were not allowed to serve in the military had worked to an extent, giving them a chance to finally compete for trophies with a 'good' roster of players.

Interestingly, this was the last World Series to be played in one stadium only, as the Cardinals and Browns shared the same stadium. This remained the case until 2020, when the World Series was played entirely in Arlington, Texas.

The Browns did have a chance to go and win the title, though, as they had won two of the first three games, so they did have a lead over the Cardinals. The final three games were also closer than others in the series, too. The fact the Browns found some success, though, and the fact they had brought in more fans than the Cardinals over the season, was seen as a success in itself. In fact, it was the first time since 1925 that the Browns had brought more fans to the stadium than the Cardinals. It would also be the last.

The 1945 season, though, was another relative failure. They finished with an 81-70 record in the league, finishing third in the table. However, the 1945 season is more famous for the fact that the team fielded Pete Gray, a player who only had one arm – this made him the only one-armed player to play in the Major Leagues in the history of the league. His one season in the Majors is a story in itself, which we have covered.

The Browns never had another winning season in St. Louis, though, and the team only enjoyed eight winning seasons in total after 1922. The team was eventually sold in the 1950s to Baltimore as already mentioned. This brought about the end of one of the most unsuccessful teams to ever stay in the Major leagues for more than a few years.

For fans of the 1944 team, though, there was finally something to shout about. Despite the reasons for getting to the World Series, the St. Louis Browns could finally say they had reached the peak of the sport. They might not have won, but for one season they had found some success at last.

CHAPTER 15
TOPPS BASEBALL CARDS BECOME A PHENOMENON

For baseball fans of all ages, a big part of the sports popularity has come down to the fact that there are so many collectibles. From sports jerseys and baseball bats, gloves, and balls themselves, there are so many things to collect. One of the biggest collectibles within baseball, though, are Topps baseball cards. You no doubt have some at home – they are a must-have!

However, at one stage in baseball, these cards were not a thing. In fact, one of the most commonly collected items in baseball only came around after the Second World War. Here is the story of how Topps baseball cards came into being, and why they are still so popular even today.

For any young baseball fan, collecting Topps baseball cards is just part of the experience. Collecting your favourite players, and the legends of the game, is just part of what being a baseball fan is all about. Something special comes from opening up those packs of cards, hoping to get that one card that you are missing to complete the set. Kids all around America trade these cards with friends, looking to complete their own collection while helping out friends to do the same.

Go back to before the Second World War, though, and this was a much rarer thing. In fact, the only companies who were producing baseball cards included bubblegum and tobacco makers. This gave the hobby some interest, but it was nowhere near as popular before the Second World War as it was in the future. In 1948, though, a company called Bowman began to produce baseball cards, and before long they started to become very popular once again.

Fans of the sport were back to collecting images of their most beloved players. Fans were able to find cards of the best players for the biggest teams, building 'dream team' collections that they would show off to friends. In 1951, though, everything changed. Why? Because the company Topps got involved in card creation.

In 1951, Topps produced their first ever collection of baseball cards. Two sets of 52 cards were created: this was to copy classic playing cards as you would use for playing something like poker. Topps cards soon became the most popular and desirable, and young kids started to collect them en masse. Everyone wanted to have their own collection and to have all of the cards.

Bowman was still creating cards, too, but in 1956 Topps decided to buy out Bowman. This meant that Topps trading cards soon became the number one choice on the market. This remained the case for almost thirty years, with Topps being the go-to choice for baseball cards all the way until 1981. Even as new competition began to arrive on the scene in the 1980s, though, Topps remained the main card producer. Kids always wanted to have their own collection of Topps cards.

Interestingly, though, Topps was not always the sure-fire success that it is today. When the company first got involved in the card business in 1951, it was seen as a failure. The full baseball set that was released by Topps at first did not take off: fans preferred the likes of Bowman baseball trading cards instead.

The original cards that were first produced were much smaller than the cards that we get today. They were designed to look like playing cards, too, with a similar design making them look more like an ace of spades than the trading cards that we get in the shops today. The cards were very basic, with only a small piece of information about the player who was on the card included as part of the design.

The two sets of cards produced at first included Red Backs and Blue Backs, with 52 of each card type available. This meant that in total 105 different players were included. This included various stars of the game such as Yogi Berra and Enos Slaughter. Cards were sold in small packs of two, costing around one penny, and at first the sales were really poor. Fans did not know what to make of the cards. What was the point?

The basic design and the small amount of information on the card meant that, for many, it was not interesting. It is strange to look at the basic old cards and wonder how it managed to evolve into the massive industry that it is today.

While sales were poor, though, they were good enough to help Topps come out with a new set in 1952. They learned lessons from the mistakes made with their first release, and the second batches of cards were much more well-loved by fans. They brought in various new designs and styles that were much more popular with the fans.

Also, the collection was much bigger – 407 cards were included as part of the 1952 collection. Players had colour photos, too, and they also provided a shot of the players autograph which made them just look a lot more authentic. These new cards were a much bigger hit, and they started to sell all around America. The back of the card also contained a lot more information about each player, so collectors could learn about their favourite players through the back of the card.

This set in stone the development for the Topps card collection, and it grew into a sensation. Over 200,000 baseball cards have since been produced in the Hall of Fame. The cards became a huge trading item for kids and for people of all ages who loved the sport of baseball. As time has gone on, baseball card collecting has become as common as actually going and watching the sport itself.

Even to this day, then, Topps still remains the #1 choice for baseball fans collecting cards. In a way, card collecting has become as popular as the sport itself. Many fans are introduced to the sport thanks to the Topps cards, or it helps them to learn more about the game. Various styles of cards exist today, but it is likely that baseball trading cards would not have become as popular as they are today without Topps.

For over seventy years, then, Topps has been one of the most important collectibles in American sports. While others might have gotten involved in the act, too, it is fair to say that Topps trading cards are still the #1 choice for fans up and down the country.

CHAPTER 16
DON LARSEN AND THE PERFECT GAME

Baseball is a sport where players dream of perfection. Every time someone steps on the field, they want to come off without making a single mistake. As any young player who has played the game will know, though, being perfect at baseball is pretty tough. Some players in history, though, have managed to play the 'perfect game' and obtain a status no other player can. One player who fits that example better than most is Don Larsen.

Don Larsen was a player who played for the New York Yankees in the 1950s, and he was a very important part of their success in this era. The Yankees were the best team in baseball at that point, and they were on a run of amazing title success brought together by legends like Yogi Berra and Larsen himself. However, even with so much success, the idea of a 'perfect game' felt so rare.

On October 8th 1956, though, that finally changed. Not only did Larsen produce a perfect game, but he did so during the 1956 World Series against the Brooklyn Dodgers. Given how big the rivalry between the Dodgers and Yankees is, this was an amazing experience for fans to see.

Before he could play his perfect game, though, Larsen had to go through a few trials. For example, Larsen was an important player for the Yankees, but he did not start every game for them. During the

World Series, he had not managed to get a starting place in the team until the fourth game of the 1955 World Series. He was given the chance to start, though, and he managed to pitch four innings. In those innings, he managed to allow five runs on five hits, and the Yankees lost the game 8-3.

The Dodgers, then, went on to win the World Series in 1955 in seven games. This was their first championship, and it left the Yankees reeling. They were not used to losing to anyone, nevermind local rivals in a World Series match-up. In 1956, though, both teams would come face to face again in the World Series.

The Dodgers took the first game of this new 1956 series, and for many Yankees fans it felt like a curse was opening up. For the second game of the series, though, the Yankees' coach, Casey Stengel, decided that he would give Larsen another start. He would be up against Don Newcombe on the other side. Larsen, though, struggled big time. The team were 6-0 up, but Larsen did not even make two innings and played his part in the team losing again – this time 13-8.

He gave up one hit, but managed to walk out four batters, which gave four runs to the team. However, the runs were invalidated due to an error made by Joe Collins. The Yankees, though, managed to rally and came back to win Games 3 and 4 of the series – this left the series tied at 2-2.

The fifth game of the series, then, would be one of the most important. Larsen started again for the Yankees, and he found himself up against Sal Maglie who had played such a big role in the 1955 victory for the Dodgers. The Yankees started fast, though, getting a pair of runs from Maglie, but for Larsen this was the beginning of an amazing, life-changing moment.

As the game went on, Mickey Mantle managed a home run in the fourth inning, while Larsen played the perfect game. He faced off against 27 different batters, and he managed to retire every single one of them – thus, he managed the 'perfect game' in the most amazing way. Incredibly, he did so using only 97 pitches, and only one single batter for the Dodgers – Pee Wee Reese – managed to land a three-ball count. Larsen played the most important game of his career, and the Yankees went on to win the game.

At the end of the game, his teammate Yogi Berra jumped up on top of Larsen to celebrate such an amazing achievement. It was one of the most amazing sights ever seen on a baseball field, and it has gone down in history as one of the single most important moments to ever take place in Yankees history. Having struggled up until this point in the series, Don Larsen made sure that he would now go down in history as one of the truly great Yankees players. Today, this is remembered as one of the most special moments to happen in Yankees history. Given how much success they have had over the years, that is saying something!

In fact, this was such a special experience that it took until 2022 for someone to do the same again. The run by Larsen was the only 'no-hitter' in the history of the World Series until a group of players playing for the Houston Astros achieved the same feat. The players in question are Cristian Javier, Rafael Montero, Ryan Pressly, and Bryan Abreu. The group of Astros all combined for a no-hitter in the 2022 World Series up against the Philadelphia Phillies.

However, Larsen remains the only player in MLB history to have hit a perfect game in the World Series. It is thus remembered as one of the most special and important moments in the entire history of the sport and league. For Yankees fans who were present that day, being able to tell their loved ones about such a sight is something they will never forget.

For a hundred years to come – or more – fans will remember the Don Larsen Perfect Game. For that reason, it is one of the most important moments in the entire history of the league. It is yet another example, too, of the Yankees being the most powerful team in the history of the sport.

While Larsen sadly passed away in January 2020, at the age of 90, he was the last remaining member of that Yankees team who played in the game. In fact, he was the last remaining player from either side. In a way, that feels fitting.

CHAPTER 17

LOU GEHRIG: THE 'LUCKIEST MAN ON THE FACE OF THE EARTH'

American sports are made for heroes. For people who give everything they have – and more – on the field of play. For players who have contributed to the growth of the sport they play. For leaving special memories that fans can remember forever. This is a big part of what makes American sports so enjoyable to watch: they have players who have changed the whole of their sport. When it comes to baseball, few players can match what Lou Gehrig achieved on and off the field.

To fans of all ages, Gehrig is a name known. Whether you are a youngster who is just getting into baseball or you have watched it for all of your life so far, you will have heard the name Lou Gehrig. From his amazing achievements in the 1930s – including playing 2,130 consecutive games of baseball, once a world record – to his trophy cabinet, Gehrig is one of the most important baseball players of all-time. He was also, in his own words, the luckiest man on the face of the Earth.

This is the story of his amazing speech, and what made him such a famous name in the eyes of so many baseball fans around the world.

Gehrig himself enjoyed an incredible career as a baseball player. He took to the field from 1923 until 1939, playing for the New York Yankees in one of their typical spells of success. In that time, he managed to achieve a great amount of success, including being a seven-time All-Star and also the Most Valuable Player (MVP) of the American League twice. On top of that, he won six World Series championships to go with his 493 home runs. He was one of the best basemen to ever play the game, and his powerful hitting and his ability to play game after game set him apart from many of the players who played in his era.

Gehrig enjoyed a legendary career, playing so many games for the Yankees and winning so many titles. On top of that, his 2,130 games in a row was believed to be unbeatable. For his era, he was the most impressive player of his time – a truly special player, a winner, and someone who could overcome anything on the field of play. He was loved away from baseball too, and like heroes such as Joe DiMaggio Gehrig was seen as one of the 'good guys' of the sports world.

However, sadly, he became impacted by a disease known as ALS, which is eventually fatal. It stops the body from moving on its own, and it was a disease that was diagnosed in Gehrig in 1939. This meant that he had to go about retiring from the sport that had given him so much. A very private person, Gehrig was not interested in talking about his retirement. However, he was asked by the team to give his speech to the crowd. His retirement came on the 19th June, 1939, and the public wanted to honour him in some way.

The Yankees retired his No. 4 jersey, and Gehrig was given July 4th as "Lou Gehrig Appreciation Day" by his old team. Some 61,808 fans turned up for his farewell appearance at the stadium. He was the first player to ever have his number retired – a practice that is still rare today, but happens for other legends of the game. On July 4th, then, he decided that it was time to retire and he gave what is still known as one of the most famous speeches in the history of baseball.

In his speech, Gehrig gave a speech that he had memorised before coming out to the field. His speech was long and impressive, and to many it is regarded as one of the best speeches ever given by an athlete in the USA. During the speech, he started by saying: *"Fans, for the past two weeks, you've been reading about a bad break. Today I consider myself the luckiest man on the face of the Earth. I have been in ballparks for 17 years and have never received anything but kindness and encouragement from you fans."*

Despite living with an illness that would be fatal eventually, Gehrig maintained a very happy outlook on the world. He was applauded by the crowd for two minutes, and he looked emotional when he finally stopped talking and sat down. His former teammate, who he had a tough relationship with at times, Babe Ruth, gave him a massive hug. Even the toughest of people in the crowd – reporters, friends, competitors, fans, everyone – felt emotional listening to this amazing speech.

For Gehrig to be able to continue to be so upbeat despite what he was going through felt like another example of why he is so loved even today by fans who never saw him play. Sadly, Gehrig passed away at the age of 37, dying on June 2nd, 1941. He was brought to the Church of the Divine Paternity in New York, where thousands gathered to pay tribute to one of the best to ever play baseball at any level.

Though he did not live the long life that he should have, Gehrig enjoyed an amazing career as a baseball player and is regarded as one of the truly great American stars of his era. His speech will go down as one of the most important memories to ever happen on a baseball field. For all of his amazing success on the field, it is his powerful speech when he was so ill that made him such an amazing person to remember.

Fans of all ages, of all teams, will always remember the legendary Lou Gehrig. From his six World Series wins to his importance to turning the Yankees into one of the biggest sports teams in the world, few people in the entire sport of baseball can say that they had the impact on the world that Gehrig did. For a time, he truly was the luckiest man on the face of the Earth.

CHAPTER 18
THE MOVE OF THE DODGERS AND GIANTS TO LOS ANGELES

L ike most American sports, Major League Baseball has seen more than a few big movements over the years. Teams have moved cities and states, and it has become common for teams to move around more than once. In fact, not many teams have stayed in their original location since they were first founded. Two of the most important teams in the history of the league, though, are the Dodgers and the Giants. Did you know, though, that both teams did not always play in California?

From their foundations in the late 1800s until the 1950s, the Dodgers and Giants played in a different city. In fact, both clubs were based in New York City as opposed to Los Angeles and San Francisco. The Giants were once based in Manhattan, while the Dodgers played their games in Brooklyn. For years, they were massive rivals right in New York – until, in the 1950s, it was decided they would move.

However, while both teams eventually arrived in California, things were nearly very different indeed. In fact, if Giants owner at the time, Horace Stoneham, had his way, then the Giants would have moved to Minnesota instead!

The idea of moving the teams to California first came up in 1957, when the Dodgers owner, Walter O'Malley, decided it was time to move. The move was not well-received. The Dodgers were one of the most popular teams in New York, and one of the most profitable teams in the baseball league. At the same time, though, Giants owner Stoneham was giving thought to moving the Giants out of town.

There were various reasons for the move, but one of the big reasons was simply to get out of the shadow of the New York Yankees. Since the Yankees acquired Babe Ruth from the Boston Red Sox, they had become the winningest team in the league. Both teams were keen to move out of the city and start afresh somewhere new, and it was decided that the Dodgers would be moved over to California instead.

The Giants had various options, too. They had looked at Minnesota, but also places like St. Petersburg in Florida. However, a meeting between the two owners decided that it was too important to the league – and to each other – to break up this amazing rivalry. Both teams, then, agreed that they would move to California.

Another big reason for the move was that the Western part of the USA did not really have any baseball presence at the time. There were no MLB teams on the western coast, and so both teams were keen to make their mark. Instead of being second to the Yankees in New York, they would be first among equals out in California. And so, the move was agreed and on the Opening Day of the 1958 season both teams faced off against each other at the Seals Stadium, San Francisco.

The Giants overcame the Dodgers to win 8-0, and thus the rivalry became even more intense than ever. Now they were competing to be the best team in California, not simply the second best team in New York behind the dominant Yankees.

At the time, the move was not without controversy or worry. However, the owners of the various MLB teams all voted and agreed unanimously with the move. The idea of having teams move around 3,000 miles west was seen as a huge controversy, and fans back in New York were heartbroken. What would they do? Could the move be stopped? Most knew that the move was permanent, and that there was nothing that could be done to stop the move.

Given that the Giants had been so successful during the early 20th Century, fans could not believe that they were being moved away. Their massive stadium, the 55,000-seater stadium, The Polo Grounds, was the envy of the league. Why would the Giants want to leave behind their famous home? What was the benefit of leaving the success and glamour of New York just to move away and start it all over again?

However, fans need to look at the history of the team from the 1940s onward. Attendances had dropped massively, and the team had finished no higher than third place in the National League for a long time. They were no longer the big team in New York, and had seen themselves fall away massively. The city of New York was also keen to regain land used by baseball teams for things like public housing.

The poor condition of the stadium in the 1950s meant that, to the city, this was an easy option. The team needed to try and make more money, and they were struggling to find ways to get success at the park. A move to a new city, a fresh start, could be just what was needed to help the Giants – and the Dodgers – win again.

The Dodgers, though, were in better shape on and off the park compared to the Giants at the time. They had a lot of good players, and were still turning a profit. The owner, though, was not happy – he wanted to build a new stadium, moving on from the old Ebbets Field, and had spent years arguing with the city about getting a new stadium. Without the money to buy the land needed for the stadium, he was eventually faced with the idea of moving out of the city and starting something new.

With so much land space in Los Angeles, then, it was seen as the ideal place to move. A city with no baseball history, but with a growing population. The L.A. Stars were bought by O'Malley, and he took the team with him after a May 28th 1957 vote within the league. Both teams, then, bid farewell to New York and moved to California where they remain today.

The San Francisco Giants and the Los Angeles Dodgers, then, are two of the most famous names in baseball. Around sixty years ago, though, they were the Brooklyn Dodgers and the New York Giants. This just goes to show how much things can change in baseball.

CHAPTER 19
THE SHOT HEARD AROUND THE WORLD

Some of the biggest moments in baseball happened a long time ago, but it was these moments that helped to make the sport as popular as it is today. Fans from all across the history of the sport have seen some amazing things happen. From legendary players to perfect games to title droughts ending, fans have seen everything happen on the baseball fields of America. However, one of the most famous moments to ever happen was The Shot Heard Around The World.

This famous moment is one of the most important in all of Major League Baseball history. The shot itself was a walk-off home run that was hit by Bobby Thomson, a third baseman for the New York Giants, from pitcher Ralph Branca of the Brooklyn Dodgers. Given that both teams were major rivals, this shot goes down as one of the most famous in the history of the rivalry. Both teams now play out in California, but during their New York days they were huge rivals.

During the 1951 season, the Giants, Dodgers, and Philadelphia Phillies were seen as the main contenders for success in the National League. The Dodgers had a huge lead as the season progressed, and it was remarked that they would be first-place winners barring a disaster in their last 50 games or so. The Phillies were soon out of the picture, leaving just the Giants capable of catching their rivals.

However, the Dodgers started to falter as many did not predict. By September 20th, they were just 4 and a half games ahead of their hated rivals. With only ten games left of the season, though, the Giants would need to win them all and hope for a miracle: the Dodgers lost six of ten, while the Giants did win all of their remaining seven games. So, both teams finished the normal season with identical records: 96-58.

At this point, a three-game playoff tie between the two teams was arranged. The first game of the series saw the Giants win 3-1 in a shock result. Home runs by Thomson and teammate Monte Irvin saw them take the game, and the second game of the series was then held at the Polo Ground.

The Dodgers won, though, tying the series, meaning that both teams would meet for one more game. The Dodgers won the second game 10-0, which was seen as setting the tone for the third and final game in the series. How could the Giants return confidently after losing by such a huge scoreline?

The game that became known as The Shot Heard Around The World took place on October 3rd, 1951, and it was a shot that won the National League pennant for the Giants. The shot came in the ninth inning of the third game in a three-game series. The Giants had trailed 4-1 going into the ninth inning, and 4-2 before Thomson stood up to bat.

The game is one of the most famous in the history of the sport, with millions across the USA watching the game on television or listening on radio. In fact, it was also played in Korea, where America was in the middle of fighting.

What makes this moment so special for Giants fans was that they were staring down the barrel of losing to their hated rivals. They had found themselves expecting to lose after being in such a bad position, and it was going to take a miracle to turn things around and win the tie once and for all. Enter Thomson.

Thomson was so important to winning the game, but not only with The Shot Heard Around The World. He also played a big part in the game, and was involved in running, fielding, and hitting equally. He was 3 for 3 at the plate, and he also managed to bat in four of the five runs made by the Giants. He managed to be a key part of taking the lead back from the Dodgers in the game, before he went on to produce his amazing home run to win the game in the ninth innings.

His ability to help complete the comeback was one of the most important moments in the history of the Giants. It also helped to make sure that Thomson would go down as one of their most important-ever players. A home run in such a moment would always make a player feel special: to beat their rivals, to go to the World Series, after all of the hard work put in to chase down the Dodgers, made it even more special.

This shot had the impact of making the rivalry between the two teams even stronger than it was, if that was possible. It also had seen the Giants win a long run of games towards the end of the season – winning 37 of 44 games – to catch-up with their hated rivals and force the playoff series in the first place. The Giants had rallied in a way that was not regularly seen in baseball at the time. Being able to come back and win the playoff series and thus go to the World Series themselves was a special moment for the team.

However, for the Giants, this victory was not one to celebrate for long. They would face off against the hugely successful Yankees in the World Series. For Giants fans, the World Series is not one to remember. They lost the series in six games to the Yankees, and were unable to keep up with them. At the end of the series, the long-term coach of the Dodgers resigned.

For Thomson, though, The Shot Heard Around The World is the shot that defines his career and his legacy as an MLB great. However, he also managed other great moments in his career, including being selected as an All-Star three times and also having eight 20-home run seasons in his career. Later in life, though, Thomson said that it was the greatest thing that ever happened 'to anybody' such was the importance of the moment.

CHAPTER 20
WHEN ROGER MARIS BEAT BABE RUTH

Like all sports, baseball is home to some amazing records that were set by players of long ago. As the sport has changed, many of its records have tumbled. The legends of the past are replaced by heroes of the modern day, and many of the 'unbroken' records have been overcome. This has always been seen as a moment where the legends of yesterday pass on the moment to the heroes of today. However, some moments in baseball history felt, for a time, like they never would be beaten. One name who has always found themselves on the outside looking in, though, is Roger Maris.

Maris was a right-fielder who played for several teams in the Major League Baseball league of the 1950s. He played 12 seasons in total in the MLB, playing for teams like the Cleveland Indians, Kansas City Athletics, New York Yankees, and St. Louis Cardinals. In his career, he achieved great success, as an All-Star from 1959 until 1962 and as the American League's Most Valuable Player (MVP) in 1960 and in 1961. He played in seven World Series events, winning three – twice with the Yankees (1961, 1962) and once with the Cardinals (1967).

However, his biggest achievement arguably came in the 1961 season when he broke a record set by Babe Ruth. That record? A record 61 home runs in a single season, which was a record that stood until

2022 when Aaron Judge broke that record. Why, though, is this record so controversial?

Given the importance of Babe Ruth to the world of baseball, anyone breaking his records has to be pretty good. At the same time, they need to be a pretty special person to be remembered as fondly as the Bambino himself. However, for Roger Maris, his record-breaking achievement came with a lot of dislike from the people at the top of the sport. In fact, many believe that the league 'never forgave' him for breaking one of Ruth's most cherished records in the game.

Ruth's single season record of 60 home runs in a season had stood for a long time, and it was seen as a record that nobody would beat. After all, nobody had ever really gotten close in the history of the game since Ruth. Maris, though, was a special player. He was a hugely successful outfielder and was seen as one of the best in his position in the world. Even someone like Maris, though, would be lucky to get close to breaking such a famous record.

On September 26th 1961, though, he got the chance to match the record set by Ruth himself. In this game, he was up against the Baltimore Orioles. The Yankees went on to win the game 3-2, and in this match Maris managed to match the home runs record set by Ruth. This was the 158th game of the season, so he was very close to running out of time to manage the award. However, he set the record for himself five days later. Some argue, though, that since Ruth did it when the season was only 154 games long, his record should still stand in many ways. It was the final game of the season when Maris finally broke the record, leading to a great amount of celebration among his teammates and Yankees fans.

However, there were arguments that the longer season and the expansion of teams meant that the record did not mean quite as much as Ruth's did when he did in a smaller league and a shorter season. The bad feeling within the league, though, never really went away – there was a degree of resentment that someone had dared to break one of the truly great runs set by Ruth.

Given Ruth's importance to the sport, many fans and experts did not like to see his records matched or broken. It was felt that it would take away from his legend to an extent, something that was often disputed by those who break his record. However, the uncertainty can be felt in the fact that Maris has never been brought into the Baseball Hall of Fame despite the amazing success that he had in his career.

In over 1,400 career games, though, Maris was a very good player. He was regularly part of All-Star teams, and was a big part of the Yankees and Cardinals winning the World Series in the three series that he did win. However, he was never given the love that other players of his era received purely because he broke the record of one of the true all-time greats.

What makes his record so impressive is the fact that, across history, very few players even came close to reaching 50 home runs in a season, nevermind 60 and above. Maris himself had stated before the 1961 season started that he could not see anyone getting near the record of Ruth. It was not a record, then, that he expected to get near or break in the long-term.

In the 1960 season, he and his teammates hit a whopping 165 home runs. Therefore, Maris came into the season believing that he was at the top form of his career and he might have had a chance at doing something special. However, the idea of breaking a record that had stood for over 30 years at that point seemed unrealistic. The record books were even suggested to have been edited to show that Ruth's record still stood, and that Maris "only" managed to do so in a longer 162-game season.

The record itself was finally broken in the modern era, and the player who broke the record, Aaron Judge, did not receive anything like the same negativity from fans of the sport. For Roger Maris, though, the success of the 1961 season – and of his wider career – was enough to be more than satisfied with.

He retired in 1968 from the sport, and spent much of his time operating a beer distribution company after his retirement. He returned to the Yankee Stadium in 1978 for the first time, and was given a standing ovation by the crowd. Maris died in 1985 after an illness, but is still remembered all of these years later as one of the truly great record breaking Yankees players.

CHAPTER 21
JOE DIMAGGIO'S 56 STRAIGHT GAME HITS

Baseball has many heroes, some who have not played for many years. Some of the greatest players in the history of baseball, after all, played almost one hundred years ago. While it might have been a long time since Joe DiMaggio played baseball, his career is one of the most legendary of all. Few players in the history of the game can come close to matching his achievements on the field. Or get close to his personality off the field, either!

Part of what makes Joe DiMaggio such a hero for baseball fans is his amazing run of records. Like the special Babe Ruth, DiMaggio has a range of records and special moments that are his and his alone. He stands alone when it comes to some of the most important achievements on the baseball field. There are many records that are never to be broken in the eyes of experts – and one record that might never come close to being broken is Joe's record of hits in 56 straight games.

Joe DiMaggio, then, is one of the greatest baseball players ever. He was a center fielder, and played his whole 13-year career in the league for the New York Yankees. He was arguably the next 'superstar' in the league, and he helped to inspire a generation of players who would come after him.

In his career, he was an All-Star in every season he played. He was also named the American League's Most Valuable Player (MVP) three times. His career was filled with success, too, including ten AL pennants and nine World Series trophies. In fact, only Yogi Berra, another Yankees legend, managed to win more World Series rings than DiMaggio did.

Some records in baseball have come close to being broken, only for the record breaker to fall short at the last hurdle. Joe DiMaggio's 56-game hitting streak, though, has never even been nearly broken. During this special run, Joe managed to hit one run and one RBI per game at least, and in the season of this achievement – the 1941 season – he only struck out 13 times.

Between the 15th May and 16th June, then, Joe DiMaggio achieved what was believed to be impossible. At the time, he batted .408 – he also slugged .717 and hit 15 homers as well as 16 doubles during this incredible run of form. It was undoubtedly one of the most special moments ever seen on a baseball field.

At 56 straight games, no other baseball player has come even within single digits of that incredible run. The next best came in 1978, when Pete Rose carried out a 44-game hit streak. That, though, was still weeks of form away from what DiMaggio had managed back in the day. Though Rose's is seen as the 'modern' record, most true baseball fans still see DiMaggio's record as the one and true record of this kind.

Another incredible fact about the DiMaggio 56-hit streak was that, in that season, he went on to hit in 17 other games safely once the streak was broken. This meant that for the season he managed to hit safely in 73 of the 74 games that he played. The schedule did not make it easier, either; he played in seven double-header games during the period.

The streak finally came to an end on July 17th of that year, when a pair of backhand stops by Ken Keltner of the Cleveland Indians brought his amazing record run to an end. The fact he managed to go on another 16-game streak right after this one ended just goes to show how amazing the form was in this season. In a career filled with amazing seasons and moments, this was probably the greatest of them all.

The streak that he was aiming to beat at the time was set by George Sisler, who had set the record at 41 games. However, DiMaggio, in his usual style, did not really seem to be too bothered about breaking the record!

In fact, he said that he would "like to get the record" only when he started to get close to the record itself. The all-time record at the time was 44, though, set by Wee Willie Keeler back in 1897. He broke this record in front of a 52,832 crowd at Yankee Stadium, and the streak simply continued from there.

Most experts believe that the record set by DiMaggio is impossible to be broken. It is seen by many to be almost impossible to do once; for someone to do it again, or break it, would be almost impossible. In fact, some have suggested that the record is the most unique thing to ever happen in American sports, so unique is the nature of this record. Despite others disagreeing, and various computer simulations creating longer streaks, nobody has come close to matching what Joe was able to do as a player.

As such, his career is seen as one of the most special of all-time. Not only did he break records for fun, but he has set records that are almost certainly never going to be broken. The way baseball is played today also means that it would be very hard indeed for someone to come along and break the streak. It simply would require too much to work in their favour.

Across his career, DiMaggio managed 361 home runs and 2,214 hits. It was a truly special run of form, and in his career – which lasted from 1936 until 1951 – he helped to set a whole new range of records. His slugging percentage of .579 is also one of the highest in the history of baseball.

Needless to say, he was brought into the Baseball Hall of Fame in 1955, and was voted as the greatest player still to be alive in a 1969 poll. Joe DiMaggio sadly passed away in 1999 at the age of 84, but it is certain that his life and career will live on forever.

CHAPTER 22
WHEN BABE RUTHS 714 WAS FINALLY BROKEN

Baseball is a sport of many records, some of which have stood for a long, long time. In fact, many of the biggest MLB records have stood for so long that it is almost impossible to imagine them ever being broken. As the saying goes, though, records are there to be broken. While some records feel like they will stand for eternity, it only takes one player to find the right moment to change history.

When it comes to Major League Baseball, all fans know who Babe Ruth is. He is the greatest New York Yankee of all-time, and one of the greatest Boston Red Sox of all-time, too. He could even be argued to be the greatest baseball player ever. His career was legendary. He achieved so much – and one of his most impressive achievements was his record of 714 career home runs. Seen as the "magic number" and a record that would never be broken, many players tried but failed.

The player who finally managed to break the record, though, was Hank Aaron. Known as "Hammerin' Hank", Henry Louis Aaron was one of the greatest baseball players of all-time. He played over 20 seasons in the MLB, playing for teams like the Milwaukee Braves (later known as the Atlanta Braves), as well as playing two seasons in the American League for the Milwaukee Brewers. In his career, he achieved many moments of success that marked him out as one of the greatest of his generation.

A powerful right fielder and designated hitter, he was seen by many as one of the first players to have a chance at breaking Ruth's amazing record. A record of 714 career home runs was, at the time, seen as a run record that would never be beaten. It was simply too high a number: who could get close to the legendary Bambino?

In baseball history, the run number that Ruth put together was one of the first 'magic numbers' in the history of the sport. Given it was such a high number, most believed that no player would be able to play to such a high level for long enough to be able to break it. However, it was an aim of Hank to finally break the record and take it for himself – and in the 1973 season he came very close indeed.

As the season continued on, Aaron came close to breaking the record but ran out of time. By the end of the 1973 baseball season, he was just two runs short of the magic number that Ruth had set. Surely, in the 1974 season, he would get the chance to finally achieve the magic number for himself?

As fans expected, in 1974 he belted in a home run on the opening day of the season. This meant that as the Atlanta Braves took on the Los Angeles Dodgers at home, he had the chance to match the record – and maybe even break it.

Sadly, at this point, in the lead up to the big game, Hank received racial abuse from fans who did not want to see him break the record of Ruth. He never, though, stopped believing that this was a record that he would finally hold for himself. In the game against the Dodgers, he found himself up against Al Downing going into the fourth inning. Hank hit a tough shot to the left field, and the shot cleared the fence – there it was, home run number 715!

The home run that he achieved resulted in a massive celebration in the stadium. Fans who were there that day can say that they have seen one of the greatest moments in baseball history. Being able to break the most magic of all magic numbers in the sport was a blessing for Aaron. It helped to set him apart from Ruth, and to put himself in the discussion of being one of the greatest players to ever play baseball. It was a special moment for him and his family, and it was a moment that he would never forget.

Given that he was coming up for age 40 at the time, too, it was a hugely impressive moment for a veteran player. Despite the threats and the abuse that were coming in towards Aaron and even to those who were covering the story, he played on. He never let anyone get in the way of breaking the record, and the massive amount of public support he received from fans around the country helped him to stay focused.

For all of the worries about racial tension, the standing ovation that was given to Aaron for his amazing performance was something that would never be forgotten. It was a moment that would live in the memories of all true baseball fans, and became one of the most iconic moments in the history of the sport as a whole. For many Americans, it is one of the greatest achievements ever seen by an athlete.

Babe Ruth is regarded as the best to ever play the game. To be able to break one of his most famous and long-standing records was just proof of how good Aaron was. The celebrations went down in history, with fireworks lighting up the sky, and fans could finally say that they had seen one of the truly special records being broken.

For Aaron, being able to break such a special record was a highlight moment in what was already an amazing career. He was given the chance to enter the Baseball Hall of Fame in 1982, the first year he was available to enter, and he was voted in. He was also entered into the Wisconsin Athletic Hall of Fame, in 1988, for his work for sports teams in the state.

In 1999, the Hank Aaron Award was created: the award is given to the hitters who are regarded as the most effective in each of the leagues per season. In a career that was filled with so much success, breaking the record of the legendary Babe Ruth probably stands out as the most impressive achievement of all.

CHAPTER 23
DISCO DEMOLITION NIGHT

Across the history of professional baseball in America, attendances have always been an issue. There have been times when full stadiums were almost guaranteed. At other stages in the history of Major League Baseball, there have been problems getting fans to come to attend matches in person. Over the years, various events have been used to try and encourage fans to come back to the stadiums to take part in the fun up-close and in-person.

This has led to many teams getting creative with how they try to get fans through the door. One such example can be found in the July 12th, 1979 'Disco Demolition' night. This event was one of the most infamous moments in MLB history, and it created what turned into a near full-scale riot. The story is one that every baseball fan should know, though, because it is one of the most surreal moments to ever happen within the world of professional baseball.

The rise of disco music in the 1960s had created a cultural divide within the country. Many people were enjoying the rise of disco, while others felt that it was simply not for them. Many feared that disco would take over from rock music entirely. For example, WKTU was a rock music radio station, but it was not rated very highly. They turned to a disco station, and in turn became the most popular radio station in the entire USA.

In the late 1970s, there was an active anti-disco movement in America, as odd as that might sound. People wanted to avoid disco music from becoming the massive chart-topper that it was becoming – they wanted old-school rock music to stick around. This gave the owner of the Chicago White Sox, Bill Veeck, an idea. Veeck had always been keen to use different promotions to try and get more fans through the door. He and his son Mike began to create ideas that would help them to bring in more fans to the White Sox games.

As Veeck looked for ways to try and get more fans to come along to the game, they came up with the idea of a 'Disco Demolition' evening – where fans would bring along disco music, and the records would literally be blown up in front of the audience. The night it was decided to do this was July 12th, 1979.

The promotion idea was simple: anyone who came along with a disco record to be blown up would get in the stadium for just 98 cents. The person who would blow up the records was Steve Dahl, a DJ for radio station WDAI. Dahl was fired on Christmas Eve in 1978 as the radio decided to move from rock music to disco. Dahl instead joined WLUIP, a rival rock radio station, and created his "Disco DIE" and "Insane Coho Lips" movements – anti-disco movements, basically.

Fans were invited to come along to Comiskey Park and have their records blown up and destroyed once and for all. However, there were fears that there was not enough public interest or traction in the event and it was going to become a big mistake. The White Sox had been seeing crowds of around 15,000 – the stadium held over 44,000. Sitting at around 40-46 on the record, too, the White Sox were by no means a winning team.

The White Sox, though, were confident that the promotion could bring in even another 5,000 or so fans, bringing the attendance up to around the 20,000 mark. However, well over maximum capacity turned up to watch the game – it is believed that an official attendance of around 47,795 was not correct. Instead, Veeck believes that anything from 50-55,000 people managed to get into the stadium for that event.

Many of the disco boxes were now overflowing, with so many records brought along by those who wanted to be part of a pretty funny event. Most of the fans who had come along had come to see the disco detonation as opposed to the actual game, so the crowd was very rowdy. As the game came to an end, the box of disco records was brought into the middle of the field. Fans who were unable to give their disco records to the staff at the stadium simply threw their disco music down into the stands. Dahl himself was asked to come out at the end of the game and take the honours of blowing up all of these disco records. He duly did so, with the game ending at around 8.16PM and the explosion happening around 8.40PM. Dahl came out, dressed in military attire and a helmet, and then took the box of records into centre field.

While some fans wished to leave, the security team had locked the gates so that nobody else could sneak into the stadium and thus create an even bigger demand for capacity. Dahl spoke to the crowd, telling them they were attending the "world's largest anti disco rally" and they set the bombs off.

To the surprise of nobody, though, the explosion caused a huge piece of damage to the outfield grass. As soon as the explosion went off, fans started to stream onto the field– well over 5,000 – and professionals still on the field ran off the field to try and get to some form of safety. Veeck stood with a megaphone trying in vain to get fans to return to their seats, but to no avail. A riot started.

At around 9PM, police turned up in riot gear and the remaining fans were escorted from the field. Around 39 people were arrested, and around 30 people were hurt during the riot. The field was so badly damaged from the explosion, that the next game with the Detroit Tigers was called off. The Tigers coach, Sparky Anderson, refused to let his players take to the field for the next game.

The White Sox, it was argued, were at fault for blowing up their own field. The second game against the Tigers was forfeited, with a 9-0 score going to the Tigers. Accused of not providing the right playing conditions, then, the White Sox found that for all of the extra fans they got for one night the damage they did to their own field and their reputation was not really worth the cost.

The White Sox ownership took a lot of criticism for the decision to hold the night, and to take the risk of blowing up the vinyl records while people were in the stadium. For fans of the MLB, the actual match itself is not very memorable – the incidents that took place, though, are going to go down as some of the most unique in the history of the sport.

With disco music beginning to die out in the early 1980s, though, Dahl and others still believe that the controversial night played a role in "killing" disco as a main music style in America. To this day, the event is still spoken about as one of the most controversial – and downright strange – to ever take place in a baseball ground. Can you imagine watching someone blow up the ground in the stadium!?

CHAPTER 24

THE LEGENDARY CAREER OF VIN SCULLY

When we think of baseball, we often think of the players and the coaches as the main attraction. For some teams, though, there are other people who become just as important to the team's history as those on the pitch or in the dugout. One such example comes in the form of Vincent Scully, or 'Vin' as he was mostly known. Vin Scully was the play-by-play announcer for the Los Angeles Dodgers (once known as the Brooklyn Dodgers).

Starting from his career position in 1950 until his retirement in 2016, Vin Scully was the voice of Dodgers games for over 60 years. He was part of the culture around the team, and he was known by fans for his excellent ability to call the game unlike any others. In fact, his career with the Dodgers is the longest of any broadcaster when it comes to staying with one team. The only person who was with the Dodgers longer than Scully was Tommy Lasorda, who was there for two years longer in total. For Dodgers fans, though, Scully is a true legend of the Dodgers franchise.

His career in broadcasting started with Fordham and CBS Radio, having left the US Navy to become a student broadcaster and journalist. Majoring in English, he was given a chance to take part in some minor radio shows, such as Fordham University's own WFUV radio station. He also played for their baseball team, the Fordham Rams, and he also called radio broadcasts for the Rams as well as for football and basketball teams.

He was hired as a fill-in by WTOP in Washington, who needed a fill-in to come in and take part. He impressed bosses with his coverage of the 1949 University of Maryland vs Boston University commentary, giving his commentary from the roof of the stadium itself. The game was a highly exciting one, and his excellent play-calling saw him get more and more opportunities.

One thing that made Scully stand out, though, was that he was never a "homer" – he always gave a factual, clear coverage of the team. Despite covering the Dodgers for all of those years, he never gave the impression of someone who was only watching one team and hoping they would win. He watched the game of baseball for the fun of it. He gave impartial advice, as was recommended by his mentor Red Barber, and he even rejected requests to give a more Dodgers-friendly tone to his reporting during games.

In 1950, then, the Brooklyn Dodgers hired him to take over along-side Barber and Connie Desmond. This was the beginning of one of the most long-running broadcasting connections in American sports history.

Scully continued to take part in the broadcasting game until he reached the age of 88, at which point it was time to retire. When he did, he retired to a standing ovation from the entire crowd. Almost every game started with the same "and a very pleasant good after-noon/evening to you, wherever you may be!" – and it became a staple for Dodgers fans tuning in to watch the game.

Despite being mostly remembered for his time with the Dodgers, Scully also did some work for football and golf for CBS Sports in the 1970s and 1980s. He also worked as a play-by-play announcer for NBC Sports in the 1980s. The World Series was also a regular occurrence for him, as he called the World Series in 1979-1982 and then 1990-1997 for CBS Radio.

His final game was an October 2nd 2016 match-up against San Francisco. His second-last home game for the Dodgers was on September 23rd 2016 against the Colorado Rockies, and he was given a tribute to his career before the game started. This included various different tributes paid by people like the Commissioner of Baseball, Rob Manfred, and the Mayor Eric Garcetti.

Two days later, Scully would get his final home game for the team on the 25th against the Rockies again. The Dodgers ended up winning the game late on, and in doing so secured the NL Western Division title. After the game, he gave a beautiful speech in which he said: "You and I have been friends for a long time, but I know in my heart that I've always needed you more than you've ever needed me, and I'll miss our time together more than I can say. But you know what? There will be a new day and eventually a new year. And when the upcoming winter gives way to spring, rest assured, once again it will be 'time for Dodger baseball'. So this is Vin Scully wishing you a very pleasant good afternoon, wherever you may be."

In 2017, the Dodgers got to the World Series for the first time for nearly 30 years. Many wanted Vin to come back and do the World Series event, including Joe Buck, the Fox Sports announcer, but Scully said no. He said that he wanted to keep a low profile, and that he had done enough World Series in his life. He did, though, take the first pitch ceremony starting at Game 2 alongside 1981 World Series winning champions Fernando Valenzuela and Steve Yeager.

The Dodgers won the World Series in 2020, and Scully was given the honour of being the narrating voice for the year-end championship documentary. Being able to follow your team around for so many years is a special experience for any sports fan. For Scully, being able to be involved in so many highs and lows with the Dodgers was part of what made his life so great. Despite missing out on another two World Series commentaries, Scully retired a happy man who had seen the Dodgers do some amazing things.

Sadly, Vin passed away in August 2022 at his home in California, aged 94. For Dodgers fans of all ages, he is a voice – and a personality – that will never be forgotten. Many of the Dodgers best moments in the sixty years that he was involved in the sport were covered by Scully – as were many of the crushing lows. For fans of the team, Scully was the voice of the Brooklyn/LA Dodgers.

CHAPTER 25

THE RISE FALL AND RISE AGAIN OF JOSH HAMILTON

Baseball is a sport that is filled with highs and lows. Players can go from being stars to being out of the team in no time. Fans get used to seeing players being stars one season only to see them being dropped completely the next year. However, one thing that is true about baseball – especially Major League Baseball – is that players can come back from even the worst situations. The speed at which the sport moves means that players can find new chances appearing all the time. One such example of this is the story of Josh Hamilton.

Hamilton was born May 21st, 1981, and he played as an outfielder from 2007 to 2015. He played most of his time in the league with the Texas Rangers. In his career, he was a 5-time All-Star, and also won awards such as the Silver Slugger Award. He was even named the Most Valuable Player in 2010. Though he never won the World Series, he did win the American League pennant twice, with the Rangers, in 2010 and 2011.

Playing in the Major Leagues, he also played for the Cincinnati Reds and the Los Angeles Angels. However, for a long time in his career, it did not look like things were going to work out for Hamilton at all!

His story is one of perseverance and overcoming challenges in life. He is one of the most inspirational players of recent years simply because he managed to make a career in the Major Leagues when everyone had written him off completely. His baseball career actually started in 1999, when he was selected by the Tampa Bay Devil Rays with the first overall pick.

Like most players who are taken with the first pick, Hamilton came into the league with a great reputation. He was seen as a great prospect, a player who had everything to make it as an outfielder.

He started his MLB career playing in the Minor Leagues, playing for teams like the Hudson Valley Renegades and the Charleston River-Dogs. Here, he played very well, and was part of the 2000 All-Star Futures match. He was voted Player of the Year in the Minor Leagues by USA Today, and his career looked like it was going to take off in a special way.

So much was his early success that his parents quit their jobs so they could travel around the country with their son. In 2001, though, everything changed for Hamilton and his family. Josh was involved in a terrible car accident, and the injuries that were caused by the incident saw him fall into a negative place. In the 2001 season, he managed to play just 45 games, as he struggled to get back into any kind of fitness. He also had some issues with alcohol and even drugs. To many, it was the beginning of the end of the career of a great prospect. Neck and toe injuries were common for him, too, meaning he was unable to really develop as a player.

He found himself suspended from the league due to a failed drug test, and he spent as many as three years outside of baseball. Rehabilitation, though, was something that he was aiming for every single day. He intended to get better, but continued to struggle with his career. In 2006, he reached the worst point – he was suspended for the entire season.

Hamilton was given a chance to change things, though, when Roy Silver, a former Minor League outfielder, gave him a shot at taking part in a baseball academy in Florida. He worked at the academy in exchange for using the equipment there, and he was eventually given the chance to play in the Minor Leagues once again. He played with the Renegades again in 2006, trying to stay fit and to get himself noticed.

Thanks to a rule known as the Rule 5 Draft, though, he was able to be selected by another team. The Chicago Cubs, this time, took a chance on the young star. He was immediately traded to the Cincinnati Reds, though. Rule 5 players are very rarely as talented as Hamilton; his injuries and personal issues, though, meant that he needed to use something like this as an opportunity to get better. He joined the Cincinnati Reds in 2007, and hit a batting average of .403 in the spring training camp. He finally made his debut in the Major Leagues, aged 26, on the 2nd April 2007. His debut came against the Cubs, and he was given a standing ovation by the crowd. He scored his first home run in the MLB against the Arizona Diamondbacks. He was named the Rookie of the Month for April, and he spent much of his first season playing center field. At the end of the year, he was traded to the Texas Rangers.

With the Rangers, he made his name – in 2009 he was voted the MVP of the League, and helped the Rangers get to the World Series. Though they lost the series, losing to the San Francisco Giants, the season was seen as a big success for the team and for Hamilton himself. The Rangers returned to the World Series in 2011, again losing, this time to the St. Louis Cardinals.

He continued to enjoy success as a baseball player, and his success continued until he was traded to the LA Angels. He played there for two years, before returning to the Rangers in 2015. He played with the Rangers until 2018, when he finally retired. Unfortunately, his career was brought to an end due to left and right knee injuries, meaning that he had to finally give up.

In nine seasons in the MLB, though, he played over 1000 games, made over 600 runs, and 200 home runs. He was eventually brought into the Texas Rangers Hall of Fame in 2019.

For many, Josh Hamilton is one of the best examples in all of baseball when it comes to overcoming challenges in life. For any kids who have been rejected, or who are struggling to be seen, use Hamilton as an example. He was more or less out of the league completely, before finally getting his big break in 2007. In the nine seasons that followed, he did enough to become a Hall of Famer for one of the league's biggest clubs.

Hamilton is one of the best examples in sport of being able to come through tough times. It might not always be easy, but it can be done. Kids, use Josh Hamilton as an example of what can be achieved when the right level of effort is put forward.

CHAPTER 26
THE RISE OF THE
KNUCKLEBALL PITCHER

For anyone who follows baseball as a sport, there are certain positions that every fan becomes aware of. For example, a pitcher is one of the most important players on the field. They are often one of the most useful people in the team when it comes to getting wins. Without a good pitcher, it is pretty hard to go on and win trophies!

That is why, for years, there has been a 'right' way to throw a baseball, and a 'wrong' way. The best pitchers tended to follow the same style. However, this set way of doing things meant that for many players it was easy to be lost in the number of quality options for hire. Good quality pitchers could find it hard to get a starting role, simply because someone else could do the same job but better.

To stand out from the crowd, pitchers have – over time – used different methods to change up their style. They have come up with new ways to throw the ball, and to help make their game generally more unique. This helps players who might not stand out from the crowd to become starting pitchers in Major League Baseball. One modern example of this comes from R.A. Dickey.

Knuckleballs are thrown in a way that ensures the has as little spin on it as is possible. This can make the ball more difficult to hit, and it can create motions that are hard for batters to deal with. Not only can this make the ball more challenging to hit for a batter, but it can also ensure that catchers struggle to even grab the ball. For many, it is a controversial style of baseball.

When knuckleballing first came to be is hard to stay for sure, but it was being used as far back as the 1908 season. For example, Eddie Cicotte, who played for the Chicago White Sox, was known as "Knuckles" due to his style of playing the game. Others, though, believe that the first 'real' knuckleballer came from Charles H. Druery. In 1917, Druery helped to show Eddie Rommel how to throw the ball in this unique way – he became a very successful player for the Philadelphia Athletics.

Knuckleball is quite a rare skill for a pitcher to learn within the world of baseball. For example, until around 20 years ago less than 70 MLB professionals have used the knuckleball as part of their skills. Knuckleballers, though, can find it hard to get into the league because the way they throw the ball means that it is often not as quick. Given scouts pay attention to the speed of a pitch from a pitcher, many knuckleballers are not seen as worthwhile by scouts.

Scouts tend to look for a player who has a faster throw, and this means that knuckleball has become very rare within the world of MLB. As the modern MLB continues to focus on power and speed, knuckleball professionals are increasingly rare. Those who do manage to throw this way, though, tend to be very hard opponents to deal with.

Three Hall of Fame players, though – Hoyt Willhelm, Jesse Haines, and Phil Niekro – have been knuckleballers. Another member of the Hall of Fame, Ted Lyons, also started to knuckleball later on in his career. During the early 1930s, an arm injury forced Lyons to change his style, and he began to knuckleball with impressive results. Phil Niekro's brother, Joe, was also a knuckleballer – this makes them arguably the only duo of brothers to be known for such a unique way of playing the game.

Why do so few players use the knuckleball? According to R.A. Dickey, it takes around one year to master this style of play. As such, many players cannot dedicate the time to learn such a unique way of playing the game. Therefore, it is hard for someone to change to knuckleball later on in their career. There are, though, some very interesting examples of players who have managed to become knuckleballers after going professional.

Another reason why many players do not learn knuckleball is that many managers and coaches do not trust it as a skill. Coaches are happy to tell a player to stop knuckleballing as soon as they make one mistake – players with a more traditional style, though, will keep getting chances to play. Most argue that you need a coach who is willing to put up with the unique style and the potential benefits that come from using knuckleball.

One highly specific example of someone using knuckleball to their advantage comes from R.A. Dickey. The pitcher has played for teams like the Texas Rangers, Seattle Mariners, Minnesota Twins, New York Mets, Toronto Blue Jays, and Atlanta Braves. He, though, had to change his entire game as he struggled in his early MLB career. His traditional pitching game was regarded as poor – so he learned knuckleball.

This forced him to adapt to a new style of play – with great rewards. In 2012, he was named to his very first All-Star team, and he also won the Pitcher of the Year award from Sporting News. He also won the Cy Young Award – the first ever knuckleballer to do so – after producing an incredible 230 strikeouts. His style was very rare, though – from changing his game in 2012 to 2017, he and Steven Wright of the Boston Red Sox were the only players using knuckleball in the entire MLB.

Given how rare it was to see someone using this particular pitching style, Dickey helped to bring back knuckleball into baseball popularity. He tended to use a slow knuckleball when he was behind in the count, but if he was ahead he would speed things up. This made him one of the most unpredictable pitchers in the league.

Today, knuckleball is still extremely rare within the sport of baseball. It is, though, a tactic that many younger players are starting to learn. As coaches become more open-minded to the idea, we might see an increased number of players using this style of play in the years to come. For any young player reading this who wants to think about trying out a knuckleball – go right ahead!

It takes practice and hard work, but it can be a very useful skill to have for any baseball pitcher. You only need to look at how many Hall of Famers have used the skill to see how useful it could be.

CHAPTER 27
CAL RIPKEN'S IRONMAN STREAK

Major League Baseball is a tough season. With so many games in one year, players often need lots of time to recover. The challenge of playing baseball for years on end is that it can become very draining on the body. For Cal Ripken Jr. though that did not seem to matter. As one of the most famous baseball players of all-time, Cal Ripken is a true legend of not only the MLB, but baseball worldwide.

Born on August 24th, 1960, Cal Ripken was born Calvin Edwin Ripken Jr. – his nickname as a player, though, was The Iron Man. Ripken grew up in Maryland, and spent much of his time traveling around the country with his father, Cal Sr.

Cal worked for the team that he would later play for, The Baltimore Orioles. Having enjoyed a successful career in high school, he joined the Orioles in the 1978 MLB Draft. By 1981, he was playing in the major leagues. In his career in MLB, he played for the Orioles, playing 21 seasons for them. He was a shortstop and third baseman and was thought of as one of the best attacking players in baseball during his career.

He played mostly as a shortstop, though he did play some time as a third base player in 1982. In 1983, though, it was time for Ripken to begin to build what would make him The Iron Man. An amazing run of consecutive games played that would eventually become the all-time record. It is almost certain never to be broken.

One thing that made Ripken stand out so much from other players was his height. At 6ft 4in, he was much taller than most players who played in his position. Thanks to the amazing work of Ripken, though, the position has become a more open opportunity for larger players to get a chance.

Across his time with the Orioles, Ripken completed an amazing 3,184 hits, 431 home runs, and over 1,695 runs batted. This has made sure that baseball fans all around the world know the name Cal Ripken. He was a great attacker, but he also won two Golden Glove Awards in his career due to his excellent defending. A real all-rounder of the game, Ripken was beloved by not only Orioles fans but baseball fans from around the world.

Arguably the best season of his career came in 1991, when he won the MVP award for his amazing success on the field that season. He also won the World Series for the Orioles, though this came earlier in his career in 1983.

In 21 seasons, he was named an All-Star 19 times, and was also the Most Valuable Player (MVP) of the league twice. By far and away the most amazing achievement of his legendary career, though, is his Iron Man streak of 2,632 games played in a row. He managed to break the record set by the heroic Lou Gehrig, who completed a streak of 2,130 games. That record stood for over 50 years!

In fact, at one point in baseball history it was assumed that nobody would ever break Gehrig's record. As Ripken got closer to the record, many assumed that he would miss a game. However, on September 6th, 1995, Ripken completed the never thought possible career streak. In fact, it was voted the most famous moment of all time in the history of the MLB!

The game, a 4-2 win against the California Angels, was a night of celebration for Orioles fans who have watched one of the best players to ever wear the jersey. Orange and white balloons were released into the sky after the final out was made. Fans celebrated, and Ripken carried out a lap in front of his beloved fans.

He continued the streak – which lasted a stunning 17 years – at 2,632 games. This was before the final home game of the 1998 Orioles season. For the last period of his career, Ripken finished his career playing as a third baseman. In fact, the streak only came to an end because Ripken decided that it was time to end the streak himself.

30 minutes before the final game of the 1998 season, Ripken visited his manager, Ray Miller, and told him that he wanted to bring the streak to an end. He wanted to end the streak in front of his own home fans, and he agreed with his wife that this was the best time for him to do it. Having played another three years consecutively after Gehrig's record was broken, Ripken ensured that he would go down as a legend.

At the end of his career, Ripken was named as part of the Baseball Hall of Fame. He was voted in with over 98% of the votes, which is one of the highest percentages ever for a Hall of Fame member. This goes to show just how much he was loved by those who watched his incredible baseball career take place. From 1981 until 2001, Ripken was regarded as one of the best to ever play.

In his playing career, Ripken was able to set some amazing records. Though he was not the most exciting player to watch, Ripken was known for being great at the basics of the game, which ensured he always played really well. Indeed, he has held all-time records at one stage for assists, putouts, and for the fewest errors made.

Another record that Ripken holds is that he and his brother Billy are just one of four brother combinations to play shortstop for the same team. Few players in the history of the sport can point to having so many unique records in their name.

So, in an amazing career, Cal Ripken managed to surpass one of the all-time greats in Gehrig. Though he believes that he was never on the same level as Gehrig, the fact he so comfortably overcame his streak means that Ripken very much deserved the title of Iron Man. For most fans of the sport, few players have made quite the impact that Ripken did on the game – there is a reason why he is a Hall of Famer, and always will be.

CHAPTER 28
THE STORY OF MARK FIDRYCH

When it comes to the sport of Major League Baseball, few players are more recognizable than Mark 'The Bird' Fidrych. Born on August 14th, 1954, Mark Steven Fidrych enjoyed a short but successful career within the MLB. For four years, he played for the Detroit Tigers, playing for them from 1976 until 1980. Though these were his only years as an MLB star, in that time he became instantly recognized.

Part of what made Fidrych so recognizable was the fact that he was quirky. While most players were stoic and serious on the field, Fidrych was a lot more happy-go-lucky than most. While injuries eventually stopped what was a very promising career, in his time with Detroit he did win the American League Rookie of the Year Award. Why, though, is he considered an MLB legend?

Most baseball players become remembered for the trophies they win or the success that they have on the field. Some, though, are remembered for the fun that they bring to the game. Fidrych, though very successful for the Tigers, very much fits in this latter category. Making his debut for the Tigers in 1976, aged only 20, he was very quickly nicknamed "The Bird" – why?

Put simply, he looked like Big Bird from Sesame Street!

Not only did he bring one of the most endearing personalities to the field, but his general look and style stood out like a sore thumb in what was a very serious, conservative league. While most who took part in playing baseball at the time looked very stoic, Fidrych was far more laid back in his style and personality. He stood very tall for a baseballer, too, which made him increasingly easy to spot for fans of the game.

Unlike other players of the time, too, he was more about accuracy and movement than he was about raw power. His antics made him a very interesting player, and in his first season he finished with a highly impressive 19-9 record for the Tigers. This helped him to win his Rookie of the Year award. His time with the Tigers was highly exciting, with some very impressive games.

For example, in 1976 he played what is known as a 'complete-game victory' and is regarded even today as one of the MLB's greatest ever moments. His personality shone through as he completed one of the most impressive individual games ever seen by a player. While it was not quite like winning the World Series, it was as close as the Tigers were going to get to that kind of atmosphere and euphoria.

Another one of the main reasons why Fidrych was so beloved by baseball fans was his hilarious style. He would get rid of old cleat marks on the pitcher's mound, saying that he was "manicuring" it. He also regularly spoke to himself, and would speak to the ball before playing. He also regularly aimed the ball almost like he was about to play darts. He would also regularly throw balls away that "had hits" within the ball, asking that they be removed from the game when playing.

As his legendary nickname showed, fans of Detroit would regularly chant "We want the Bird!" towards the end of home games. He would usually emerge from the dugout to give the crowd some love. While today such antics are really much more common, it was thanks to the likes of Fidrych that baseball became less serious.

At the time, he regularly appeared on the cover of sports magazines and entertainment magazines like Rolling Stone. Part of what made Fidrych so famous, too, was his ability to just be a normal person. Having admitted that he would have been happy working at a gas station if he never made it as a pro, he never became overly serious. Though his career was cut short due to injury, he is well-remembered today both by baseball and his old team, the Detroit Tigers.

His appeal meant that the league benefited massively, with attendances skyrocketing as fans wished to see one of the most humble and unique baseball players in the game. Sadly, regular injuries had meant that his game was never enjoyed by fans for as long as he should have been able to. Undiagnosed injuries and other issues meant that, by the age of 29, he had to retire from even minor league baseball.

However, this never damaged his happy-go-lucky mannerism and style. He retained an upbeat personality and was regularly involved in the media, such was the demand to find out what one of the most interesting MLB players of his era was doing with his life.

Sadly, Fidrych died in April 2009 when an incident with his dump truck saw him die in a horrible accident. Thousands of people turned up to celebrate the life of one of the most exciting and energetic characters to ever make it as a baseball professional.

While his career came to an abrupt end and his life too, even today Fidrych is remembered by those who saw him play. For true lovers of baseball, the name Mark Fidrych transcends his already very impressive record as a baseball player. For most, he was beyond that of just a normal player – he was one of the most unique people to ever take part in a professional game of baseball.

Today, he is remembered fondly by fans of all teams. Fans of the sport will always remember that 1976 game against the Yankees, when he produced a performance so majestic that fans refused to go home until he came out for a standing ovation.

From his exciting personality and his true love of baseball to his incredible ability and accuracy, Fidrych cemented his position as one of the best baseball players of all-time. Though his career only lasted a short while, in that time he managed to make an impact so big that fans are still talking about his greatest moments close to 50 years after they first took place.

CHAPTER 29
THE STORY OF WADE BOGGS

n sports today, fans are always told about the high levels of commitment that players need to stay healthy. To look after their bodies, they cannot eat the same foods as a 'normal' person. They need to eat a very strict, clearly focused diet. Why? Because otherwise, they will not be in the best condition to play their sport. Baseball, though, is a sport of outliers. Of people who break the typical expected rules. And when it comes to breaking the dietary commitments of a superstar, Wade Boggs does it better than most!

Born June 15th, 1958, in Omaha, Nebraska, Wade Boggs was born to be a star without even knowing it. In his career, he enjoyed incredible success. In his career, he played with the Boston Red Sox, New York Yankees, and the Tampa Bay Devil Rays. Across 18 seasons in Major League Baseball, Boggs played as a third baseman and was one of the best in the business.

Indeed, he made over 3,000 career hits and was a regular contender for the batting titles handed out during the season. Indeed, his batting average stands within the top 40 for all MLB players who have reached a minimum of 1,000 plate appearances. If you break it down to those who are still living, he has the best ranking of them all!

Part of the Devil Rays and Red Sox Hall of Fame, Boggs stood out because of his incredible playing style. To those watching, you would assume that Boggs was one of the most dedicated professionals of his era. His consistency and a near-20 year career on the field ensured that Boggs would always be remembered as one of the very best baseball players of his generation. A 12-time All Star, too, Boggs left his mark on the game and has been rated within the Top 110 Greatest Baseball Players by groups like *Sporting News*.

So, it would be fair to say that Boggs is known for his outstanding commitment to the game of baseball. Making his debut on the 10th April, 1982, he played for the Boston Red Sox for ten years, before joining the Yankees in 1993 and playing for them until 1997. He finished his career with a one-year stint playing for the Devil Rays. A World Series champion with the Yankees in 1996, he also was the winner of the Golden Glove award in 1994 and in 1995. His #26 and #12 jerseys are retired in Boston and Tampa Bay, respectively, and he was a first-ballot Hall of Fame addition in 2005.

So, now you know why so many people love Wade Boggs. He was an incredible player. Someone who was beloved by teams, teammates, fans, and media alike. However, what really makes Wade Boggs stand out is his rather more blasé attitude to life away from baseball!

Being able to score 3,010 hits in a career is very impressive. What makes Boggs so impressive to many, though, is the otherwise normal life that he lived away from the baseball world.

Part of his legend and mystique comes from the fact that he enjoyed a rather strange pre-match ritual. Before games, he was immensely superstitious and believed that he needed a combination of two things to succeed: chicken, and Miller Lite beer!

Boggs was regularly seen eating copious amounts of chicken before the matches that he played. As such, it did not take him long to become known as "The Chicken Man" by teammates and eventually fans alike. His desire to eat massive amounts of chicken before playing became almost legendary within the sport itself. It helped to really mark him out as somewhat different from most of his competitors.

Now, today, it would be almost ridiculous for an athlete at MLB level to be eating so much chicken before a game. For this particular Hall of Famer, though, it was almost a necessity to help make sure he could play to the level that he knew he could!

When asked about why he became known as The Chicken Man in

an interview in 1985, Boggs noted: "`It started in '77. I had a minor league budget and a growing family to feed. Chicken was cheap and I really felt better eating lighter food rather than a lot of heavy meat and gravy. Then I noticed my batting average going up. Ever since I've been a `chicketarian.'"

In fact, it was common for him to eat an entire chicken by himself before the game. On top of that, he would follow extremely specific training and practice regimes: he would start his batting practice at 5:17, and then sprints at 7:17 before taking to the baseball field. Superstition is a huge part of athletic life, and for Boggs it was the kind of important distinction that helped him stand out among his peers.

Part of that superstition, though, was the previously mentioned love of beer. While athletes today almost certainly DO NOT drink beer before they head out on the field, Boggs was always happy to have a few cold ones before he would start playing!

Miller Lite was his drink of choice, and he became famous for his desire to have a pretty significant amount of beer prior to playing. In fact, one legendary story that has been relayed more than once is the claim that he drank as many as *sixty four* beers on a flight across the country for an MLB game.

However, Boggs himself has denied that the number of beers was quite as high as 64 – he did, though, note that he had 'a few' on this particular trip. From game to game, though, Boggs loved to drink a few beers.

Despite a diet and a beer craving that would almost certainly not pass muster today, then, Boggs is remembered as one of the best baseball players of his generation. With some amazing statistics behind his famous career and a very upbeat and nonchalant attitude, Wade Boggs is loved by baseball fans for a great many reasons!

CHAPTER 30

THE STORY OF MORDECAI "THREE FINGER" BROWN

American sports has always been a place for heroes. Where we can go and watch the best people in each sport rise to the top of the world. To give us something to remember for the rest of our lives. Some stars, though, shine brighter than others. In the case of Mordecai "Three Finger" Brown, not many stars have shone brighter!

You might not know who Three Finger is. Born on October 19th, 1876, Brown was born to mother Jane and father Peter and grew up in Nyseville, IN. He grew up in a big family, too – seven brothers and sisters. Life in the Brown household was very busy indeed.

For young Mortimer or Mort, though, life was fun. The home was busy, but the family loved one another, and they enjoyed their days. At the age of 7, though, Mort was in an accident. His hand was caught in a corn shredder when visiting an uncle. He lost his index finger, leaving him with only four fingers on his right hand. The danger was not over, though; a few weeks later, Mot fell while running and broke every finger in his right hand!

His hand did not heal as it should, and he was left with a middle finger that was badly bent out of place. At the same time, his little finger was left paralyzed. This is where he gained the famous nickname "Three Finger" from – despite having four and a half fingers, of course, but why let facts get in the way of a good nickname, right?

Despite all of these trials and tribulations, Mort retained his love for baseball. Given his new injuries, though, he had to learn how to throw the ball – and bat – differently. Mort stayed in school until the 8th Grade when he left to find work to support his family. That's right, in the 1870s, it was common for kids in the 8th and 9th grades to get jobs.

Working in various jobs – including in the local mines of Nyesville – Mort started to play baseball semi-professionally. Typically playing at third base or as a pitcher, he stood out as one of the best players in the region despite his injuries.

In 1901, though, he joined the Terre Haute Hottentots. There, he helped them win their local league and get a promotion to the Western League. This was a much higher level of challenge, but at his new team, Omaha, he shone. Despite his injuries, Mort was so important to Omaha, winning an impressive 27 games.

At this point, his life changed – he was brought to the major leagues in 1903 by the St. Louis Cardinals!

A single season with the Cardinals was enough to show that, three fingers or not, Mort was one of the best players at this level. He was traded to the famous Chicago Cubs, joining the best team in the league at the time. Over the next six seasons, Three Finger and the Cubs won more games than any other team – he also helped the Cubs win the World Series in 1907 and 1908. Not bad for someone with a busted hand, huh?

The Cubs still hold a record that stands today – the best winning percentage in a single season of any team beyond the 1900 season. With a record of 116-36 in 1906, the Cubs set a league record of a .763 winning percentage. Amazing!

From 1906 until 1911, then, Three Finger set himself apart as one of the best players in baseball. Even with his injury, he found a way of playing that ensured he was always among the best players. He was special – unique. In 1912, though, Mort was traded to Cincinnati. This is where things began to fade.

Mort was slowing down, but in 1915 he enjoyed a great season – his last truly amazing season as a professional. In 1916, he played his final game in the major leagues at the ripe old age of 39. He continued to play the game he loved until 1920, when he retired at 43.

At this point, he returned to where it all began – Terre Haute in the Three-I League. As coach of his original boyhood team, Mort set about improving the record to bring them back to the success they enjoyed when he was a player. He remained here as a coach for a period before buying a Texaco gas station in Terre Haute. He continued to own the station until he died in 1948.

What made Three Finger so special? How did we play so well with his injury?

That is a question that has been asked a thousand times! Despite his disfigured hand, Mort was one of the best pitchers of his generation. It is claimed that he has the best curveball of any player of his generation. He was able to throw extremely hard from the break but also ensured the ball dipped quickly enough that it was hard for the opposition to stop.

His hand injury meant that Mort had to come up with a unique way of throwing the ball. This forced him to snap quickly with the ball while keeping his wrist bent. It was a unique throw, unmatched by anyone else in the league, and it meant that Three Finger was one of the hardest players to play against. For this reason, he finished with some of the best career statistics of any pitcher of his era.

Even with such a severe injury and life-changing challenges, Mort "Three Finger" Brown achieves his career dream of playing baseball. He won the World Series twice, was able to find a unique shot that suited his hand condition and was a specialist in the big games.

There are few better examples in this world of someone who has overcome a big challenge. If you ever feel like you might not be able to do something the same way as everyone else, remind yourself of Mortimer "Three Finger" Brown. He had to do things his way, which led to one of the best pitching careers in baseball history!

Made in United States
Cleveland, OH
08 June 2025

17578402R00056